Questions and Answers About
Starting a Bible Study Group

MW01035895

PURPOSE	1. *What is the purpose of a Bible study group?* Three things (and all three are important):
	a. Nurture—to be fed by God and grow in Christ, principally through Bible Study.
	b. Support—getting to know each other in a deeper way and caring for each other's needs.
	c. Mission—reaching out to non-churched people who are open to studying the Bible and reaching beyond your initial number until you can split into two groups ... and keep multiplying.
NON-CHURCHED	2. *How can people who don't go to church be interested in studying the Bible?* Pretty easy. In a recent survey, the Gallup Poll discovered that 74% of the people in America are looking for a spiritual faith.
TURNED-OFF	3. *Then, why don't they go to church?* Because they have a problem with the institutional church.
SEEKERS	4. *What are you suggesting?* That you start a Bible study group for these kinds of people.

• People who are turned off by the church but are looking for a spiritual faith.

• People who are struggling with personal problems and need a support group.

• People who are crippled by a bad experience with the church and want to start over in their spiritual pilgrimage.

• People who are down on themselves and need encouragement to see beyond their own shortcomings.

• People who are looking for hope in the face of seemingly insurmountable difficulties.

• People who flashed across your mind as you read over this list.

RECRUITING	5. *How do I get started?* Make a list of the "honest seekers you know" and keep this list on your refrigerator until you have asked everyone.
FIRST MEETING	6. *What do we do at the first meeting?* Decide on your group covenant—a "contract" that spells out your expectations and rules (see the center section, page C5).
DEVELOPING A CONTRACT	7. *How do we develop a contract?* Discuss these questions and ask someone to write down what you agree upon. (This "contract" will be used again at the close to evaluate your group).

• What is the purpose of our group?

• What are the specific goals?

• How long are we going to meet? (We recommend 13 to 26 weeks. Then if you wish to continue, you can renew the contract.)

• Where are we going to meet?

• What is going to be the starting and ending time at the sessions?

• What about refreshments/babysitting, etc.?

LIFECYCLE	8. *How long should a Bible study group last?* This should be taken in stages. (See flow chart below)

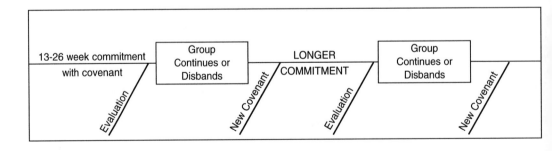

REVELATION

LOOKING AT THE END OF TIME

PROJECT ENGINEER: Lyman Coleman, Serendipity House

WRITERS FOR NOTES: Richard Peace, William Cutler

WRITERS OF GROUP QUESTIONS: The Serendipity Staff

TYPESETTING: Sharon Penington, Maurice Lydick, John Winson, Douglas LaBudde

PUBLISHER: Serendipity House is a resource community specializing in the equipping of pastors and church leaders for small group ministry in the local church in the English speaking world. A list of training events and resources can be obtained by writing to the address below.

SERENDIPITY GROUP BIBLE STUDY

Serendipity House / P.O.Box 1012 / Littleton, CO 80160

TOLL FREE 1-800-525-9563

©1995 Serendipity House. All rights reserved
98 99 / **301GBS series•CHG** / 6 5 4 3 2 1

SHORT-TERM COMMITMENT	9. *Why only a few weeks to start with?* Because people will give priority to something if they know it's not for long. And they can always renew and keep going if they wish.
STUDY PLANS	10. *How do we go about the study of this book of the Bible?* This should be decided at the first meeting. Inside the front cover of this book are two options that you can choose from. You need to discuss these options and agree on your study plans.
HOMEWORK	11. *Is there any homework?* No—unless you want to do some research about a particular concern. If you are studying one of the longer books of the Bible, where you do not have time to cover every passage, you may want to combine units, as suggested in "Course Options" and answer only one set of questions per session.
BIBLE IGNORANCE	12. *What if we have people in the group who know nothing about the Bible?* Great. This is what this group is all about. There are NOTES on the opposite page to refer to if you have any questions about a word, historical fact or significant person in the passage.
NOTES	13. *Who wrote these Notes?* Richard Peace, a Professor at Gordon Conwell Seminary and a recognized Bible scholar, and Bill Cutler, a student of Richard Peace.
SERENDIPITY	14. *What is Serendipity?* A small research company that specializes in programs for small groups in a church.
DREAM	15. *What is your dream?* Christian small groups for hurting and struggling people inside and outside of the church—built around a study of Scripture and care for one another. For further information, we invite you to call: TOLL FREE 800–525–9563, IN COLORADO 303–798–1313.

Introduction to
REVELATION

Apocalyptic Literature

The book of Revelation is unique. It is the only apocalyptic book in the New Testament. What makes this so unusual is that while the New Testament books were written, apocalyptic literature flourished. In fact, during the period between the Old and New Testaments, apocalyptic literature was the most common type of Jewish religious writing.

At the heart of apocalyptic literature was hope—hope that God would right wrongs and rescue the righteous. The Jews knew that they were God's chosen people, yet they had been subject to ungodly rulers for so long. As a result, they longed for that great day when God would intervene in history and bring about what he promised. They gave shape to these longings in the so-called apocalyptic writings (apocalypse is a Greek word meaning an "unveiling" or "uncovering" of future events or hidden realms, like heaven).

Apocalyptic literature dealt with the details of God's return: how he would burst into history, whom he would destroy, how he would set up his kingdom. These books were, of necessity, the products of dreams and visions. Consequently, they were filled with swirling images and vivid pictures of death, supernatural places and creatures, destruction and redemption, and so on. Since the events described were unlike anything that had ever happened, they could only be alluded to, often in cryptic language. The resulting mystery surrounding such writing was further compounded by the need for secrecy. Were these books to fall into the hands of the rulers (the ones singled out for destruction), they would be considered seditious and would land their authors in jail or worse. So the books were written in code. They could be understood only by those on the writer's side who had the key to the code. Outsiders, such as the police, would find them unintelligible. Of course, this is why we have a problem today in deciphering apocalyptic literature. In many cases, we have lost the key.

The Apocalyptic World View

Underlying both Jewish and Christian apocalyptic literature was the view that history is divided into two ages. The present age is evil and corrupt and it will be destroyed. The age-to-come is characterized by goodness and by God's presence and power. The central turning point in history, on which apocalyptic writers often focused, is the Day of the Lord, when the present age will give way to the new age.

Christian writers understood this to be the day of Christ's return—the Second Coming. He had come once, as a baby in Bethlehem, and by his first coming had set in motion the events that would draw the present age to a close. When he came again, it would not be as an infant but as a king before whom the whole creation would bow. For the moment, however, Christians live in the in-between time. Christ's ultimate victory was secured at the Cross; Satan was defeated. But the victory had yet to be claimed in its fullness. Satan still pretended that he was in charge and would do so until the Second Coming.

What is striking is how similar the pattern is in Christian and Jewish apocalyptic literature. Beyond the obvious difference over the role of Christ, the same outline is found in Jewish literature as in Revelation. Specifically:

1. The Messiah will be the central figure in the Day of the Lord.

2. The coming of the new age will be preceded by a terrible time in history filled with war, famine, and calamity of all sorts. In fact, the elements themselves will disintegrate, and hatred and anger will prevail in human affairs.

3. The Day of the Lord will be the time when judgment is rendered.

4. Following judgment, there will be a time of great peace and joy. The New Jerusalem will descend. The dead will rise and the Messiah will reign.

Characteristics

Not only is Revelation strange; it is also difficult. The world of the book of Revelation is so remote from the modern world that one hardly knows where to begin in trying to understand it. It is a world filled with weird beasts who have ten horns and seven heads; a world of seals and trumpets and bowls that bring disaster; a world populated with angels and demons, with lions and lambs, with horses and dragons. Who can make sense out of all this?

As a result, we often either ignore Revelation or distort it. Barclay calls Revelation "the playground of religious eccentrics" (*The Revelation of John: Daily Study Bible*, Vol. 1, p. 1). Indeed some wild notions have been extracted from Revelation and claimed to have divine sanction.

On the other hand, as Philip Carrington has said:

> In the case of the Revelation we are dealing with an artist greater than Stevenson or Coleridge or Bach. St. John has a better sense of the right word than Stevenson; he has a greater command of unearthly supernatural loveliness than Coleridge; he has a richer sense of melody and rhythm and composition than Bach ... It is the only masterpiece of pure art in the New Testament (*The Meaning of Revelation*, pp. xvii,xix).

The book of Revelation is well worth reading, but it must be approached with humility and caution. To pin one's whole theology on details in the book of Revelation is dangerous indeed. With prayer and patience, the reader needs to work at understanding the text.

Revelation is written in the worst Greek of any book of the New Testament. There are mistakes in grammar and stylistic errors such as a schoolboy would make. Yet R. H. Charles, an expert on apocalyptic literature, considers the bad grammar deliberate. According to Charles, John wrote this way for emphasis. His clumsy Greek style reflects his attempt to translate Old Testament passages—the author was thinking in Hebrew but writing in Greek. Furthermore, a vision such as John had can never be adequately captured by mere words. John had to push language to its limits even to approximate what he had seen. The poor Greek may also have resulted from John's imprisonment on Patmos, where he probably had no secretary to smooth out his style (*A Critical and Exegetical Commentary on the Revelation of St. John: International Critical Commentary*, pp. x–xi).

Author

Although the author only refers to himself as "John" (1:4), it has traditionally been assumed that he was none other than John the apostle. In fact, this simple designation "John" is strong proof in itself that the apostle was the writer. Typically, apocalyptic literature claimed to be authored by famous heroes of the past (e.g., Abraham, Ezra, Enoch, and Baruch). But John writes in his own name, and only a person of the stature of an apostle could expect to have such a work received as authoritative. Furthermore, when Revelation is compared to the Gospel of John and the three letters of John, there are striking similarities in ideas, theology, and language.

John wrote from the island of Patmos, a rocky, barren island in the Aegean Sea (10 miles long and five miles wide), where he had been exiled because of his Christian witness. Tradition says that he was eventually released from Patmos and spent the remaining years of his long life in Ephesus.

Date

Most scholars feel that the book of Revelation was written toward the end of the reign of Domitian, that is, around A.D. 90–95. This is what Irenaeus, a second-century bishop, claimed. Still, this dating is not conclusive. Evidence has been offered that it might have been written during the last years of Nero's reign (between A.D. 65 and 68) or when Vespasian was emperor (A.D. 69–79).

Audience

The book of Revelation was addressed to seven churches in the western part of the Roman province of Asia (see map). The order in which these churches are addressed is the order in which a messenger from Patmos would come to each church if he followed the great circular Roman road connecting the cities.

Theme

Rome is a central and consistently negative image in the book of Revelation. This view of the Roman government stands in contrast to the rest of the New Testament, where Rome is seen as the protector of Christianity. In the early days of missionary activity, Roman judges protected Christians from Jewish mobs (Acts 18:1–17; 19:13–41). It was Roman justice to which Paul turned in his time of need (Acts 23:12–35; 25:10–11). As a result, the apostles urged submission to Rome (Rom. 13:1–7; 1 Peter 2:13–17). But in Revelation, the attitude is quite different. Rome is seen as a whore, drunk with the blood of Christians (17:5–6), deserving nothing but destruction.

This shift in attitude is due to one thing—Caesar worship. Although Roman rulers were long considered divine, their centrality in Roman civil religion was not enforced until the end of the first century. Then it became obligatory for citizens all across the Roman Empire to appear once a year before a magistrate to burn a pinch of incense and declare, "Caesar is Lord." This was more an act of loyalty to Rome than a religious statement, but Christians simply could not bring themselves to declare that anyone except Jesus was Lord. As a result, they were hounded mercilessly by civil authorities. This is the situation to which Revelation speaks. It attempts to

encourage Christians by giving them the long view. They may suffer now while Caesar pretends to be Lord, but ahead lies unimaginable glory when Jesus, the true Lord, comes in power. This kind of vision would give harassed Christians the strength to endure.

Structure

John begins with a description of the vision from which the Book of Revelation came (chapter 1). Chapters 2 and 3 contain specific messages to seven churches in Asia Minor. Chapters 4 and 5 describe a vision of God and of Christ. Then in Chapters 6–19 various plagues of judgment are described. The book is concluded (chapters 20–22) by a description of the coming kingdom.

While the overall structure is clear, how it all fits together varies with the reader's interpretive posture.

Interpretation

There are widely varying ways to interpret Revelation. Some limit its meaning to the first-century struggle between the church and Rome. Others see Revelation as a collection of symbols that predict future events (e.g., the locusts from the bottomless pit represent the invasion of Europe by Islam). In fact, the book of Revelation probably speaks both to the immediate first-century struggle of Christians and to the future when the Lord will return.

For further discussion regarding the interpretation of the book of Revelation, please refer to the section "Author's Notes" at the back of this book on page 84.

The Seven Churches of Revelation

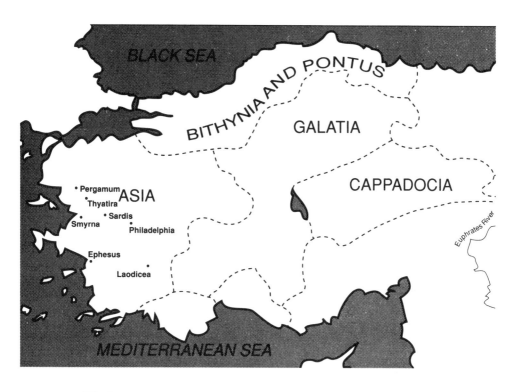

- Ephesus
  - Smyrna
    - Pergamum
      - Thyatira
        - Sardis
          - Philadelphia
            - Laodicea

UNIT 1—Prologue/Greetings and Doxology / Rev. 1:1–8

Scripture

Prologue

1 *The revelation of Jesus Christ, which God gave him to show his servants what must soon take place. He made it known by sending his angel to his servant John, [2]who testifies to everything he saw—that is, the word of God and the testimony of Jesus Christ. [3]Blessed is the one who reads the words of this prophecy, and blessed are those who hear it and take to heart what is written in it, because the time is near.*

Greetings and Doxology

[4]John,

To the seven churches in the province of Asia:

Grace and peace to you from him who is, and who was, and who is to come, and from the seven spirits[a] before his throne, [5]and from Jesus Christ, who is the faithful witness, the firstborn from the dead, and the ruler of the kings of the earth.

To him who loves us and has freed us from our sins by his blood, [6]and has made us to be a kingdom and priests to serve his God and Father—to him be glory and power for ever and ever! Amen.

[7]Look, he is coming with the clouds,
and every eye will see him,
even those who pierced him;
and all the peoples of the earth will
mourn because of him.
                    So shall it be! Amen.

[8]"I am the Alpha and the Omega," says the Lord God, "who is, and who was, and who is to come, the Almighty."

[a]4 Or *the sevenfold Spirit*

Group Questions

Every group meeting has three parts: **(1) To Begin** (15 minutes) to break the ice; **(2) Read Scripture and Discuss** (30 Minutes); and **(3) To Close and Pray** (15–30 Minutes). Try to keep on schedule. The most important time is the prayer time.

TO BEGIN / 15 Minutes (Choose 1 or 2)

❏ What vivid dream (or nightmare) from childhood do you still recall?
❏ What type of book or movie do you like best: Adventure? Science fiction? Fantasy? Historical documentary? Biography? Why?
❏ How well do you handle horror films with lots of special effects? Why?

READ SCRIPTURE AND DISCUSS / 30 Minutes

❏ Although it's a unique book in the Bible, what was obvious to the people during the time it was written (see Introduction)? Where was John when he wrote it (Author)? To whom was the book addressed (Audience)? Why is Rome portrayed negatively (Theme)?
❏ What are the five stages of "transmission" of this book (vv. 1,4)?
❏ To believers suffering severe political, religious, physical and economic oppression because of their faith, what aspect of the Gospel would be especially important?
❏ If the book of Revelation were dropped from the Bible, what would be missing from the story of God's redemptive work in history?
❏ What pressures can make you feel like giving up on Jesus? What truths about God keep you going?
❏ To some, Jesus is a baby or an innocent victim of crucifixion. To John, Jesus is the reigning King. How could this view of Jesus affect your day-to-day dealings with sin? With discouragement? With opposition? With apathy?
❏ Why did you decide to join this study? To get the most out of Revelation, what will you put into it? What do you expect from the group (think about study, prayer, shared leadership, outreach, confidentiality, accountability, etc.)?

TO CLOSE AND PRAY / 15–30 Minutes

❏ If you had a spiritual check-up today, what would the doctor prescribe?
❏ Who do you know who might like to join this group?
❏ How can this group pray for you in the coming week?

Notes

1:1–8 The prologue consists of an introduction (1:1–3) stating the origin of the work, and a salutation (1:4–8) with greetings (vv. 4–5a), a doxology (vv. 5b–6), and two prophetic sayings (vv. 7–8).

1:1–3 John identifies the five stages of transmission of this book: from Father to Son to an angel to John to the reader.

1:1 *The revelation.* Literally, *apokalupsis*—an unveiling or uncovering of something that was hidden; supernatural truths that could not be known had God not spoken them. This is the name that has been given to a type of literature that flourished in John's time, dealing with the details of the unseen spiritual realm and their implications for history (e.g., the book of Enoch). *of Jesus Christ.* This is not "the revelation of John" as the book is sometimes called; it is the testimony borne by Jesus Christ. He is the witness (v. 4). It was given to John. This phrase "implies that Jesus Christ himself has torn back the curtain which hides from human eyes the invisible world and the future of this world, and that what is open to view is a vision of reality granted by him" (Beasley-Murray). *soon take place.* Though this revelation has to do with events at the end of time (as becomes clear as the book unfolds), it also concerns events taking place in the first and second century.

1:3 Since this is a book that came straight from God (as the words "revelation" and "prophecy" imply), those who read it are especially blessed. *Blessed.* This is the first of some seven beatitudes in Revelation (see 14:13; 16:15; 19:9; 20:6; 22:7,14). *reads/hears.* This probably refers to the first-century practice of reading aloud in church. *prophecy.* This is the second word that defines what kind of book this is (the first being "revelation") Prophecy is a vision given by God of what lies ahead in both the immediate and long-term future.

1:4–8 Even though the book has been defined as "revelation" and "prophecy," it is set in the form of a letter. In a fashion typical of Greek letters, the sender and recipients are named (v. 4) and a greeting is offered (vv. 4–5).

1:4 *seven churches.* These seven churches are named in 1:11. There were other churches in this region, however (see Acts 20:5–6; Col. 1:2; 4:13). Why only these seven are addressed is not clear. They may have been the key churches in each of seven postal regions in Asia. Certainly the number seven was important (it represented perfection) and is used often in Revelation. The seven churches were located on a circular road about 30 to 50 miles from each other. *province of Asia.* The western half of Asia Minor (the western part of modern Turkey). *him who is, and who was, and who is to come.* A paraphrase of the name of God in Exodus 3:14–15. *the seven spirits.* This may be an unusual way of speaking about the Holy Spirit (the number seven referring to a complete manifestation of the Holy Spirit). Or it could refer to the seven archangels in Jewish tradition; or it could refer to seven angels who minister to the Lamb (4:5; 5:6).

1:5 Three titles are given to Jesus. *faithful witness.* Jesus is the one whose life made God known to the world. The Greek word for witness (*martys*) becomes "martyr" in English, and certainly in Revelation death is often the result of faithful allegiance to God (as it was for Jesus). *firstborn from the dead.* But Jesus did not remain dead; he rose again to become the sovereign Lord over the church. *ruler of the kings.* He is also the supreme ruler of the whole earth (Phil. 2:10–11). This assertion contradicted, of course, the first-century fact that Rome ruled without rival. Domitian (who was probably emperor when John wrote) asked to be addressed as "Lord and God." But, in fact, it is Jesus who is the ruler behind rulers and will be revealed to be so at his second coming. *To him who.* The first of several doxologies honoring Jesus (e.g., 4:11; 5:9,12–13; 7:10).

1:6 *kingdom and priests.* The early church felt itself to be the true Israel, with all the promised blessings applying to it (see Gal. 3:28; Phil. 3:3; 1 Peter 2:5,9).

1:7 When Jesus returns all will see him (not just Israel); all will mourn him (as they realize that judgment is coming).

1:8 *Alpha and Omega.* The first and last letter in the Greek alphabet. God controls the whole sweep of history. *says the Lord God.* This is one of the two places where God speaks directly (see 21:5–8).

UNIT 2—One Like a Son of Man / Revelation 1:9–20

Scripture

One Like a Son of Man

⁹*I, John, your brother and companion in the suffering and kingdom and patient endurance that are ours in Jesus, was on the island of Patmos because of the word of God and the testimony of Jesus. ¹⁰On the Lord's Day I was in the Spirit, and I heard behind me a loud voice like a trumpet, ¹¹which said: "Write on a scroll what you see and send it to the seven churches: to Ephesus, Smyrna, Pergamum, Thyatira, Sardis, Philadelphia and Laodicea."*

¹²*I turned around to see the voice that was speaking to me. And when I turned I saw seven golden lampstands, ¹³and among the lampstands was someone "like a son of man,"ᵃ dressed in a robe reaching down to his feet and with a golden sash around his chest. ¹⁴His head and hair were white like wool, as white as snow, and his eyes were like blazing fire. ¹⁵His feet were like bronze glowing in a furnace, and his voice was like the sound of rushing waters. ¹⁶In his right hand he held seven stars, and out of his mouth came a sharp double-edged sword. His face was like the sun shining in all its brilliance.*

¹⁷*When I saw him, I fell at his feet as though dead. Then he placed his right hand on me and said: "Do not be afraid. I am the First and the Last. ¹⁸I am the Living One; I was dead, and behold I am alive for ever and ever! And I hold the keys of death and Hades.*

¹⁹*"Write, therefore, what you have seen, what is now and what will take place later. ²⁰The mystery of the seven stars that you saw in my right hand and of the seven golden lampstands is this: The seven stars are the angelsᵇ of the seven churches, and the seven lampstands are the seven churches."*

Group Questions

Every group meeting has three parts: **(1) To Begin** (15 minutes) to break the ice; **(2) Read Scripture and Discuss** (30 Minutes); and **(3) To Close and Pray** (15–30 Minutes). Try to keep on schedule. The most important time is the prayer time.

TO BEGIN / 15 Minutes (Choose 1 or 2)

❑ How often do you remember your dreams? Do you dream in color?
❑ What bizarre dream can you still recall, and why?
❑ What is your favorite painting of Christ?

READ SCRIPTURE AND DISCUSS / 30 Minutes

❑ If you had a dream and saw a "son of man" like the one here, would you be afraid, awestruck or baffled?
❑ What's significant about John's spiritual condition and the day when he received this vision? (See 1:9)
❑ Close your eyes and have someone read verses 12–18 again slowly. Meditate on it. What do the images suggest about Christ? How does this make you feel?
❑ What is the meaning of the seven stars? The seven lampstands? What does it mean for a church to be a light?
❑ Using the analogy of a lighting fixture to describe the spiritual condition of your church, what kind would be most descriptive (a chandelier, a night light, etc.)? What would help to create more illumination in the church? In your life?

TO CLOSE AND PRAY / 15–30 Minutes

❑ In your spiritual life right now, are you "on Patmos" (suffering, feeling exiled) or "in the Spirit" (reigning) or experiencing both at the same time? Why?
❑ How do you feel about sharing with this group? What would you like them to understand about your expectations?
❑ Did you invite anyone to join this group?
❑ What would you like the group to pray with you about this week?

ᵃ13 Daniel 7:13   ᵇ20 Or *messengers*

Notes

1:9–20 The first vision (1:9–3:22) begins with John's account of his vision of the exalted Christ, during which he receives his commission to write this book.

1:9 John writes as one who has paid the price of being a Christian, following the example of his Lord. Thus he knows exactly what his readers are going through. *suffering.* The tribulation that comes from being a Christian (John 16:33) which will intensify during the last days before the full establishment of God's kingdom. *Patmos.* A small island in the Aegean Sea off the coast of modern Turkey; probably a Roman penal colony.

1:10 *the Lord's Day.* The first day of the week (Sunday) when Christians met to worship together because it was on this day that Jesus rose from the dead. *in the Spirit.* A trance, an ecstatic experience; a type of mystical experience (see also Acts 10:10; 11:5; 22:17; 2 Cor. 12:2–4).

1:11 The churches are named in geographical order as one went around the circular road on which they were located. *"Write on a scroll."* It is John's job to translate this vision into a written manuscript. As he does so, he will quite naturally draw upon those words, phrases and pictures which are a part of his background. This will include abundant OT imagery.

1:12 *seven golden lampstands.* These stand for the seven churches (1:20). They are a fit symbol for the church which is meant to be a light to the world (Matt. 5:14–16). *someone "like a son of man."* This phrase is from Daniel 7:13. It is a title which was rather vague (it could mean simply "a human being"), but it also had messianic overtones. Because it was vague Jesus used it for himself, filling it with new meaning and content (see Mark 8:31–10:45). It became Jesus' most common title for himself.

1:13 *dressed in a robe.* Jesus wore the full-length robe of a high priest. In 1:1–20, Jesus is presented in the threefold office of prophet (v. 1), priest (v. 13), and king (v. 5).

1:14–16 A series of divine attributes ascribed to Christ. They convey the sense of an otherworldly visitor who possessed great power, wisdom, and authority (see Dan. 7:9).

1:16 *sword.* The sword that issues from the mouth of Jesus represents the fact of divine judgment (see 2:16; 19:15, 21; Isa. 4:9; Heb. 4:12). *His face was like the sun shining.* The shimmering glory of Jesus recalls the parallel experience on the Mount of Transfiguration (Matt. 17:2).

1:17 John's response to this numinous vision of Jesus is like the response of OT prophets in similar circumstances (see Josh. 5:14; Isa. 6:5; Ezek. 1:28; Dan. 8:17; 10:15). *placed his right hand on me.* Jesus thus commissions John to undertake the task of writing what he has seen in this vision (v.19). *Do not be afraid.* These words from Jesus would have been familiar to John. He heard them on the Sea of Galilee (Matt. 14:27) and at the Mount of Transfiguration (Matt. 17:7).

1:18 *the Living One.* He possesses in his essential person Life itself, in contrast to the dead gods that populated the Roman world. *the keys.* To possess such keys means that he has the power and the authority over these realms.

1:19 Some scholars take the threefold statement in this verse to be the outline of the book of Revelation. John is to write what he had seen (i.e. the vision of the Son of Man; 1:9–20), what was then and there the state of the church (which he will do in chapters 2 and 3 via the seven letters to seven churches), and what is yet to come (which comprises the rest of the book).

UNIT 3—To the Church in Ephesus/Smyrna /Pergamum/ Thyatira / Revelation 2:1–29

Scripture

To the Church in Ephesus

2 *"To the angel[a] of the church in Ephesus write:*

These are the words of him who holds the seven stars in his right hand and walks among the seven golden lampstands: [2]I know your deeds, your hard work and your perseverance. I know that you cannot tolerate wicked men, that you have tested those who claim to be apostles but are not, and have found them false. [3]You have persevered and have endured hardships for my name, and have not grown weary.

[4]Yet I hold this against you: You have forsaken your first love. [5]Remember the height from which you have fallen! Repent and do the things you did at first. If you do not repent, I will come to you and remove your lampstand from its place. [6]But you have this in your favor: You hate the practices of the Nicolaitans, which I also hate.

[7]He who has an ear, let him hear what the Spirit says to the churches. To him who overcomes, I will give the right to eat from the tree of life, which is in the paradise of God.

To the Church in Smyrna

[8]"To the angel of the church in Smyrna write:

These are the words of him who is the First and the Last, who died and came to life again. [9]I know your afflictions and your poverty—yet you are rich! I know the slander of those who say they are Jews and are not, but are a synagogue of Satan. [10]Do not be afraid of what you are about to suffer. I tell you, the devil will put some of you in prison to test you, and you will suffer persecution for ten days. Be faithful, even to the point of death, and I will give you the crown of life.

[11]He who has an ear, let him hear what the Spirit says to the churches. He who overcomes will not be hurt at all by the second death.

[Scripture and questions continued on page 16]

Group Questions

Every group meeting has three parts: **(1) To Begin** (15 minutes) to break the ice; **(2) Read Scripture and Discuss** (30 Minutes); and **(3) To Close and Pray** (15–30 Minutes). Try to keep on schedule. The most important time is the prayer time.

TO BEGIN / 15 Minutes (Choose 1 or 2)

❏ Who was your "first love" in elementary school?
❏ Who was one of your favorite teachers growing up? Why?
❏ What teacher in high school or college did you have a hard time with? Why? Teaching style? Personality? Expectations?

READ SCRIPTURE AND DISCUSS / 30 Minutes

❏ On your first reading, does this passage seem to have anything to say to churches today, or does it feel out of date?
❏ What good things characterize the church in Ephesus? How might its strengths have been the cause of its failure? What do you think their Sunday worship was like?
❏ What is repentance? Why is that necessary for the Ephesian church?
❏ Which of the positive qualities of the church in Ephesus describe your church?
❏ In what ways have you lost your first love for Christ? What has helped you to keep that love alive?
❏ In verses 8–11, what problem is the church in Smyrna facing? How can they be both poor and rich?
❏ What does this passage teach about suffering?
❏ In verses 12–17, what pressures are the Christians in Pergamum facing? At what point are they strong? Where are they tempted? Which do you think is easier to endure: Persecution by enemies or seduction by the culture? Why?
❏ Why is the title by which Christ reveals himself so appropriate to these Christians?
❏ What is the significance of the sword (v. 16)? Of the manna and stone (v. 17)?
❏ What cultural influences distract you from your relationship with Christ? Which are subtle? Which are direct? What weapons has God given you for battle?
❏ In verses 18–28, what are the strengths of the church in Thyatira? Its weaknesses?
❏ What does the symbolic name "Jezebel" reveal about the woman in this church?

[a]1 Or *messenger;* also in verses 8, 12 and 18

Notes

2:1–3:22 The second part of this first vision consists of seven letters to the seven churches which are the focus of this letter (vv. 4,11). The letters are similar in form. Each is prefaced with a word to the angel of the church; each then begins with a descriptive phrase about Christ chosen from the titles of Jesus in the opening vision (1:13–18); each passes judgment on the church. The aim of these seven letters is to impress upon the church as a whole the need for endurance in the face of the coming persecution.

2:1 *the seven stars/the seven lampstands.* In each case, the phrase chosen is appropriate for the church in view. Here Jesus is the one who holds control over the seven angels and he walks among the seven churches. He has come to inspect his church. *the church in Ephesus.* More is known about this church than any other in the first century. One of Paul's letters is addressed to it (though Ephesians is probably a circular letter also intended for other churches in the region); it is the church that is the focus of 1 and 2 Timothy; and it is the church John addresses in his first epistle. It is also mentioned prominently in Acts (see Acts 18:18–22; 19:1–20:1; 20:17–38). Ephesus was the most important city in Asia at that time, with more than a quarter-million people living there.

2:2 *hard work/determination.* These words define the nature of the "deeds" noted by Christ in his inspection of the church. This was a church known for its deeds of goodness done in the name of Christ. "Determination" can be translated as "patience," and refers to their willingness to endure the hostile reactions of those around them. Ephesus was a city dominated by the famous temple of Diana (the mother goddess of Asia), so it is not surprising that the church had great opposition (see Acts 19:23–20:1). *tested those.* They did not reject out of hand those who came to them. They "tested the spirits" (as John had urged them in 1 John 4:1) and found these false apostles wanting. They are commended for their willingness to maintain their orthodoxy. *claim to be apostles.* In 1 Timothy, Paul dealt with the problem of false teachers in the Ephesian church (see also Acts 20:29). Apparently the church had taken his words to heart and rid themselves of these errant individuals.

2:4 Jesus turns from commendation to complaint. Despite their good works, their patient endurance and their maintenance of orthodoxy, they have fallen away from the fervor of their first love. It is not clear whether this is love for Jesus or love for others, but it is probably both since the two are connected. Such Christianity is cold and grim without the enlivening of love.

2:5 The antidote to such coldness is twofold: remembrance and repentance. If they recall what they were once like—how they loved Christ and each other—this will give them the insight they need so as to see how they have strayed. Repentance is the next step. It is deciding to turn away from the way of coldness and embrace once again the way of love. Such a decision to change, however, must be followed by activity. Thus John says, "do the things you did at first." *remove your lampstand.* "Without love the congregation ceases to be a church" (Mounce).

2:6 *Nicolaitans.* It is hard to say for certain who these individuals are. They are some sort of heretical sect who mixed Christianity and pagan practices such as idolatry and immorality. In any case, these are the false apostles whom the church had rejected.

2:7 Each letter ends with a challenge. To those who heed these words, eternal life is promised. *churches.* The plural is significant. These words are not intended only for the church at Ephesus but as a challenge to all churches.

2:8 *Smyrna.* A beautiful city some 35 miles north of Ephesus on the eastern shore of the Aegean Sea. *the First and the Last.* Smyrna had strong ties to Rome. The imperial cult, with its emperor worship, was strong there. It is not surprising therefore that Jesus reminds them that he alone is sovereign.

2:9 *afflictions.* This is a church under siege. *poverty.* It is not by accident that persecution and poverty are linked. It would have been difficult for Christians to find good jobs in a city where there was such hostility. Furthermore, their shops might have been boycotted; it is even possible that their houses were plundered. *say they are Jews.* This is meant in the

[Notes continued on page 17]

To the Church in Pergamum

¹²"To the angel of the church in Pergamum write:

These are the words of him who has the sharp, double-edged sword. ¹³I know where you live—where Satan has his throne. Yet you remain true to my name. You did not renounce your faith in me, even in the days of Antipas, my faithful witness, who was put to death in your city—where Satan lives.
¹⁴Nevertheless, I have a few things against you: You have people there who hold to the teaching of Balaam, who taught Balak to entice the Israelites to sin by eating food sacrificed to idols and by committing sexual immorality. ¹⁵Likewise you also have those who hold to the teaching of the Nicolaitans. ¹⁶Repent therefore! Otherwise, I will soon come to you and will fight against them with the sword of my mouth.
¹⁷He who has an ear, let him hear what the Spirit says to the churches. To him who overcomes, I will give some of the hidden manna. I will also give him a white stone with a new name written on it, known only to him who receives it.

To the Church in Thyatira

¹⁸"To the angel of the church in Thyatira write:

These are the words of the Son of God, whose eyes are like blazing fire and whose feet are like burnished bronze. ¹⁹I know your deeds, your love and faith, your service and perseverance, and that you are now doing more than you did at first.
²⁰Nevertheless, I have this against you: You tolerate that woman Jezebel, who calls herself a prophetess. By her teaching she misleads my servants into sexual immorality and the eating of food sacrificed to idols. ²¹I have given her time to repent of her immorality, but she is unwilling. ²²So I will cast her on a bed of suffering, and I will make those who commit adultery with her suffer intensely, unless they repent of her ways. ²³I will strike her children dead. Then all the churches will know that I am he who searches hearts and minds,

and I will repay each of you according to your deeds. ²⁴Now I say to the rest of you in Thyatira, to you who do not hold to her teaching and have not learned Satan's so-called deep secrets (I will not impose any other burden on you): ²⁵Only hold on to what you have until I come.
²⁶To him who overcomes and does my will to the end, I will give authority over the nations—

²⁷'He will rule them with an iron scepter;
he will dash them to pieces like pottery'ᵇ—
just as I have received authority from my Father. ²⁸I will also give him the morning star. ²⁹He who has an ear, let him hear what the Spirit says to the churches.

ᵇ27 Psalm 2:9

- ❏ How does Jesus describe himself? How do you interpret this description? What is he saying about himself? Why is this appropriate for the church at Thyatira?
- ❏ How is the nature and source of the temptation in Thyatira like (and unlike) that in Pergamum?
- ❏ What does Jesus' promise in verses 26–27 mean?
- ❏ Which of the qualities in verse 19 apply to you this week? Why?
- ❏ Who, or what, has played a role similar to Jezebel in your life (names aren't necessary)? How? How did the Lord free you from that influence?
- ❏ What do you appreciate most about the promise to overcomers in this section? Why?

TO CLOSE AND PRAY / 15–30 Minutes

- ❏ What are you beginning to appreciate about this group as you study Revelation together?
- ❏ If God appeared to you in a dream tonight, what do you wish he would talk to you about?
- ❏ How can this group pray with you and for you this week?

Notes (Continued)

sense of Romans 2:28–29, where Paul distinguishes between those who are Jews outwardly and those who are Jews inwardly.

2:11 The promised reward is that the overcomers will be unhurt by the second death. ***second death.*** "A rabbinic term for the death of the wicked in the next world" (Mounce).

2:12 ***Pergamum.*** Located some 40 miles north of Smyrna and 10 miles inland from the Aegean Sea, the city sat atop a thousand-foot high cone-shaped hill. It was the site of a famous library. ***double-edged sword.*** The sword was the symbol of the Roman proconsul who had the power of life and death over people. Jesus reminds them that such power is, in fact, ultimately his, not the ruler who is persecuting them.

2:13 ***where Satan has his throne.*** Pagan religion flourished in Pergamum. Four gods were worshiped there including Zeus, for whom a spectacular altar had been built jutting out from the top of the mountain (some identify this as the throne of Satan) and Aesculapius, the god of healing, who was called the Savior and whose symbol was the serpent (some see this as the reference to Satan). Pergamum was also the official center of emperor worship in Asia, with temples dedicated to Augustus and Trajan. Since Rome had become the center of Satan's activity (as will become evident as Revelation unfolds), this is probably what is meant by this phrase.

2:14 ***Balaam.*** The reference is to the OT story in which Balaam advised the Moabite women to seduce the Israelites into leaving their God (Num. 31:16; 25:1–3). Balaam became the symbol of those teachers who promote compromise with the culture and so lead the people away from true religion.

2:17 ***hidden manna.*** Manna was the supernatural food given to the Israelites during their wanderings in the wilderness. This heavenly food stands in sharp contrast to the unclean pagan food that some of the Balaamites had been feasting on. ***white stone.*** It is by no means clear what this refers to. It might refer to the white stone which gave admission to a banquet, with the allusion here being to the messianic banquet and the manna.

2:18 ***Thyatira.*** Thyatira was southeast of Pergamum. It was a manufacturing and marketing center, with numerous trade guilds. Lydia, the seller of purple, was from Thyatira (Acts 16:14ff). ***Son of God.*** Both Apollo Tyrimnos (who was worshiped here) and the emperor (who was seen as Apollo incarnate) were called the sons of the god Zeus. By his title, Jesus reminds the church that he alone is the true Son of God.

2:20 ***tolerate.*** Even though the church was growing in love and service, they allowed false teaching to exist. Unlike the Ephesians, who tested the teachers and rejected those who were false, those in Thyatira refused to deal with the matter of Jezebel. ***Jezebel.*** The original Jezebel was the wicked wife of King Ahab who promoted the worship of Baal (1 Kings 16:29–33; 2 Kings 9:30–37). Her first-century counterpart played the same role in the church; i.e., the promotion of false practices. ***prophetess.*** Prophecy was highly valued in the NT church. While it included the idea of predicting the future (Acts 11:27), it mainly involved the application of God's truth. Jezebel claimed to be this kind of inspired teacher and some in the church followed her. ***food sacrificed to idols.*** The trade guilds were pagan in orientation, requiring participation in meals of food dedicated to idols. To refuse to participate would have great economic consequences, since it would have been difficult to work without being a member of one of the guilds.

2:22–23 ***her children.*** Although some think this refers to her actual children, it is more likely that it refers to those who wholeheartedly support her teaching. Their penalty is far more severe than "those who commit adultery with her."

2:24 ***Satan's so-called deep secrets.*** She claimed to lead people into the deep things of God, but was actually introducing them to the mysteries of Satan.

2:26 ***does my will.*** The way to be an overcomer in their hostile environment is not to give in to it, but to continue in the way and works of Christ until the end.

UNIT 4—To the Church in Sardis/Philadelphia/ Laodicea / Revelation 3:1–22

Scripture

To the Church in Sardis

3 *"To the angel[a] of the church in Sardis write:*

These are the words of him who holds the seven spirits[b] of God and the seven stars. I know your deeds; you have a reputation of being alive, but you are dead. [2]Wake up! Strengthen what remains and is about to die, for I have not found your deeds complete in the sight of my God. [3]Remember, therefore, what you have received and heard; obey it, and repent. But if you do not wake up, I will come like a thief, and you will not know at what time I will come to you.

[4]Yet you have a few people in Sardis who have not soiled their clothes. They will walk with me, dressed in white, for they are worthy. [5]He who overcomes will, like them, be dressed in white. I will never blot out his name from the book of life, but will acknowledge his name before my Father and his angels. [6]He who has an ear, let him hear what the Spirit says to the churches.

To the Church in Philadelphia

[7]"To the angel of the church in Philadelphia write:

These are the words of him who is holy and true, who holds the key of David. What he opens no one can shut, and what he shuts no one can open. [8]I know your deeds. See, I have placed before you an open door that no one can shut. I know that you have little strength, yet you have kept my word and have not denied my name. [9]I will make those who are of the synagogue of Satan, who claim to be Jews though they are not, but are liars—I will make them come and fall down at your feet and acknowledge that I have loved you. [10]Since you have kept my command to endure patiently, I will also keep you from the hour of

[Scripture continued on page 20]

[a]1 Or *messenger*; also in verses 7 and 14   [b]1 Or *the sevenfold spirit*

Group Questions

TO BEGIN / 15 Minutes (Choose 1 or 2)

❑ When were you on a winning team?
❑ When were you on a losing team that worked itself up and tried again?
❑ What group have you been in that had a reputation far better than its performance?

READ SCRIPTURE AND DISCUSS / 30 Minutes

❑ What is the contrast between reputation and reality in Sardis? What dangers exist for Christians who rely on an image, instead of nurturing a genuine spiritual life?
❑ What is the only hope for the survival of the church in Sardis?
❑ If Jesus addressed the "wake-up call" in verse 2 to you, what would he want you to strengthen?
❑ How is the church in Philadelphia able to persevere? Describe their enemies. How does their reward (v. 12) fit their faithfulness?
❑ What open doors has Christ placed before you (v. 8)? How have you taken advantage of the path ways he's made available to you?
❑ What are some closed doors he's placed in your career? Your social life? Your schooling? How have you responded?
❑ In what ways are you like the Christians in Philadelphia? Unlike them?
❑ What does the "faithful and true witness" see when he looks at the Laodicean church? How does the church view itself? Why the contrast?
❑ What does Jesus tell them to do in verse 18? Why? What does this say about true wealth?
❑ How would you describe Christ, based on what you have read so far in this book? How does this expand the picture of Jesus in the Gospels?
❑ If Jesus took your spiritual temperature today (v. 15), what would he find? Why?
❑ What is Jesus waiting for at the door of your life right now? What room in your life is not open to Jesus?

TO CLOSE AND PRAY / 15–30 Minutes

❑ Since joining this group, how have you felt encouraged in your spiritual life?
❑ How would you like this group to pray for you this week?

Notes

3:1 Sardis. Sardis was located 50 miles east of Ephesus atop a 1,500-foot citadel. It had once been a powerful city, but by the first century it had lost much of its influence. Its chief value as a city lay in the fact that several major roads met there and that it was the place where the art of dyeing wool began. **reputation of being alive.** The church at Sardis was thought to be vital and full of life. **you are dead.** But, in fact, it was spiritually dead. "Here is a picture of nominal Christianity, outwardly prosperous, busy with the externals of religious activity, but devoid of spiritual life and power" (Ladd).

3:2 Wake up! This is the first of five commands. The presence of these commands means that it is possible for this church to come back to life. This particular command means "Be watchful" and may refer, in the historical context, to the fact that despite the nearly perpendicular walls of the citadel, twice the town had fallen to its enemies due to a lack of watchfulness. "As in history, so in life, to consider oneself secure and fail to remain alert is to court disaster" (Mounce).

3:3 Remember. They are to recall what they have "received and heard," i.e., the foundational facts of the Gospel and the infilling Holy Spirit which gave life to them in the first place. **repent.** Having recalled the facts of the Gospel and determined that they want to build their lives on this basis, they must then decide to turn around from the errant way in which they have been going (and which leads to death) and follow once again that path which leads to life. **like a thief.** Christ will come to them unexpectedly ("like a thief") in judgment.

3:4 a few people. Not all at Sardis have lost a vital faith. Some are still faithful. **not soiled their clothes.** In a place like Sardis, where making and dyeing wool cloth was a central occupation, the reference to clothing is appropriate. The image of soiled garments hints at the problem in Sardis. Sin of some sort (dirt) had been allowed to stain the church. **dressed in white.** The image of white garments is used elsewhere in Revelation: the Laodiceans are told to buy white garments to cover their nakedness (3:18); the 24 elders have white garments (4:4); the martyrs are given white robes (6:11); a great crowd stands before God dressed in white garments washed in the blood of the Lamb (7:9,13); the army of heaven is dressed

in white (19:14). White garments are, apparently, the dress of heaven.

3:5 book of life. The image is of some sort of divine ledger in which the names of the people are written. This picture was first found in the OT (see Ex. 32:32–33; Ps. 69:28; Dan. 12:1). In the first century, the names of citizens were recorded in a register. To have your name removed was to lose your citizenship.

3:7 Philadelphia. This was the newest of the seven cities. It was located 28 miles southeast of Sardis in a region of severe earthquakes. **him who is holy and true.** Both names were titles for God. the **key of David.** A symbolic way of speaking about the one who controls access to the royal house; in this case, the messianic kingdom (see Isa. 22:22).

3:8 open door. The meaning of this image is not certain. It might refer to the great opportunity for outreach and mission which is afforded to Philadelphia, by virtue of the fact that it is situated at the junction of trade routes which flow into the major cities of the east (see 1 Cor. 16:9). Probably it refers back to the image of Jesus as the keeper of the key for the door into the messianic kingdom of God. **little strength.** The congregation is apparently small and without much impact on the city. **have kept my word.** Yet in the recent persecution, they did not deny Jesus.

3:9 the synagogue of Satan. There has been conflict between the church and synagogue at Philadelphia, probably over the question of who were the people of God (see note for 2:9). One day those of the synagogue will acknowledge that the church is loved by God.

3:10 hour of trial. The church at Philadelphia will have to face persecution by Rome. They are promised that Christ will shield them during this terrible period. This phrase also looks ahead to the tribulation and testing that will precede the establishment of Christ's kingdom on earth at the Second Coming (see Dan. 12:1; Mark 13:14–19; 2 Thess. 2:1-12; Rev. 13:5–10).

3:11 I am coming soon. The coming of Christ to Ephesus (2:5), Pergamum (2:16), and Sardis (3:3) would be in judgment of some sort. However, his

[Notes continued on page 21]

Scripture (Continued)

trial that is going to come upon the whole world to test those who live on the earth.

¹¹I am coming soon. Hold on to what you have, so that no one will take your crown. ¹²Him who overcomes I will make a pillar in the temple of my God. Never again will he leave it. I will write on him the name of my God and the name of the city of my God, the new Jerusalem, which is coming down out of heaven from my God; and I will also write on him my new name. ¹³He who has an ear, let him hear what the Spirit says to the churches.

To the Church in Laodicea

¹⁴"To the angel of the church in Laodicea write:

These are the words of the Amen, the faithful and true witness, the ruler of God's creation. ¹⁵I know your deeds, that you are neither cold nor hot. I wish you were either one or the other! ¹⁶So, because you are lukewarm —neither hot nor cold—I am about to spit you out of my mouth. ¹⁷You say, 'I am rich; I have acquired wealth and do not need a thing.' But you do not realize that you are wretched, pitiful, poor, blind and naked. ¹⁸I counsel you to buy from me gold refined in the fire, so you can become rich; and white clothes to wear, so you can cover your shameful nakedness; and salve to put on your eyes, so you can see.

¹⁹Those whom I love I rebuke and discipline. So be earnest, and repent. ²⁰Here I am! I stand at the door and knock. If anyone hears my voice and opens the door, I will come in and eat with him, and he with me.

²¹To him who overcomes, I will give the right to sit with me on my throne, just as I overcame and sat down with my Father on his throne. ²²He who has an ear, let him hear what the Spirit says to the churches."

Notes (Continued)

coming to Philadelphia will be a great joy, in that this will signal the end of the tribulation and the beginning of life in his kingdom.

3:12 *I will write on him.* "The impact of the threefold inscription is to show that the faithful belong to God, hold citizenship in the New Jerusalem, and are in a special way related to Christ" (Mounce).

3:14 *Laodicea.* A wealthy city, situated at the intersection of three major roads, known for its banking and industry. Paul wrote a letter to this church which, unfortunately, has been lost (Col. 4:16). Like the church at Sardis, this church seems to be prosperous and without persecution or heresy. ***Amen.*** The word "amen" was used in the OT as an acknowledgment that something was true. Jesus is the one who is truly true and therefore can be relied upon.

3:15 *neither hot nor cold.* Laodicea was located near both Hierapolis (which had hot springs with mineral-laden water thought to promote healing) and Colossae (which had streams of cold, pure water). The church "was providing neither refreshment for the spiritually weary, nor healing for the spiritually sick. It was totally ineffective, and thus distasteful to its Lord" (Rudwick and Green quoted in Mounce).

3:16 *lukewarm.* By the time the hot water got to Laodicea from the springs at Hierapolis six miles away, it was tepid. ***spit you out of my mouth.*** Literally, "vomit." Lukewarm, mineral-filled water was probably so foul tasting that one would be tempted to spit it out. This church made Jesus sick.

3:17 This image would be meaningful in this city with a thriving banking system. The church was affluent and without a sense of need. This was its problem. It failed to distinguish between material and spiritual affluence. ***poor, blind, and naked.*** This picture of the church stands in sharp contrast to the everyday world of Laodicea which was known for its wealth, its eye salve, and its luxurious clothing.

3:18 In fact, they need the very products which they think they already possess. ***gold.*** Thinking themselves "rich" (v. 17), they will become truly rich only with the spiritual gold they can get from Christ. ***nakedness.*** A startling image for a people who lived in a city famous for its textile industry. At Laodicea, they raised sheep which produced a glossy black wool that they made into a famous black fabric. What the church has need of, however, are the white garments of heaven (see Note for 3:4). ***salve.*** Laodicea was the site of a famous medical school. One of its well-known products was an eye ointment. Thinking themselves clear-sighted, they need, in fact, a spiritual salve to restore their sight.

3:19 Rebuke and discipline is an expression not of hatred but of love (see Prov. 3:11–12; Heb. 12:5–6). ***love.*** The Greek word used here is *philein*, which is the kind of warm and tender affection one feels toward family members. ***repent.*** Once again, the call is to repentance (see 2:5,16; 3:3). They must turn away from their lukewarmness.

3:20 This verse is often used (legitimately) to call those without faith into relationship with Christ. In fact, in this context the call is to those within the church to return to the Lord from whom they have turned away. Repentance (v. 19) is demonstrated when Christ is invited into individual lives. Note that it is Jesus who offers to come back to them in fellowship if only they will open the door to him. ***eat with him.*** Sharing a meal was a sign that a bond existed between people. "It was a symbol of affection, of confidence, of intimacy" (Ladd).

3:21 In this final word to overcomers, Christ declares they will reign with him in his coming kingdom.

3:22 For the seventh and final time the reader is reminded of the fact that although these words are addressed to specific churches, they are also addressed to all churches. Thus the church at large has been warned against the dangers of losing its first love (Ephesus), the fear of suffering (Smyrna), doctrinal compromise (Pergamum), moral compromise (Thyatira), spiritual deadness (Sardis), failure to hold fast (Philadelphia), and lukewarmness (Laodicea) (Walvoord).

UNIT 5—The Throne in Heaven / Revelation 4:1–11

Scripture

The Throne in Heaven

4 *After this I looked, and there before me was a door standing open in heaven. And the voice I had first heard speaking to me like a trumpet said, "Come up here, and I will show you what must take place after this." ²At once I was in the Spirit, and there before me was a throne in heaven with someone sitting on it. ³And the one who sat there had the appearance of jasper and carnelian. A rainbow, resembling an emerald, encircled the throne. ⁴Surrounding the throne were twenty-four other thrones, and seated on them were twenty-four elders. They were dressed in white and had crowns of gold on their heads. ⁵From the throne came flashes of lightning, rumblings and peals of thunder. Before the throne, seven lamps were blazing. These are the seven spirits of God.ᵃ ⁶Also before the throne there was what looked like a sea of glass, clear as crystal.*

In the center, around the throne, were four living creatures, and they were covered with eyes, in front and in back. ⁷The first living creature was like a lion, the second was like an ox, the third had a face like a man, the fourth was like a flying eagle. ⁸Each of the four living creatures had six wings and was covered with eyes all around, even under his wings. Day and night they never stop saying:

> *"Holy, holy, holy*
> *is the Lord God Almighty,*
> *who was, and is, and is to come."*

⁹Whenever the living creatures give glory, honor and thanks to him who sits on the throne and who lives for ever and ever, ¹⁰the twenty-four elders fall down before him who sits on the throne, and worship him who lives for ever and ever. They lay their crowns before the throne and say:

> *¹¹"You are worthy, our Lord and God,*
> *to receive glory and honor and power,*
> *for you created all things,*
> *and by your will they were created*
> *and have their being."*

Group Questions

TO BEGIN / 15 Minutes (Choose 1 or 2)

- ❏ What is the most memorable storm you have ever been in? What happened?
- ❏ What is the biggest church, palace, or castle you've ever been in? How did you feel while inside?
- ❏ What inspires you with more awe of God—a spectacular outdoor scene or a majestic indoor atmosphere of worship?

READ SCRIPTURE AND DISCUSS / 30 Minutes

- ❏ Imagine yourself in this scene. What do you see? Hear? Feel? What impresses you about God?
- ❏ Where does this scene actually take place: In the afterlife? In some perfect order of things after this world has passed away? Or on the level of spiritual reality here and now (as in Eph. 2:6), where good and evil are unmasked to be seen for what they really are?
- ❏ Who is the figure on the throne? What is he like? What qualities do the 24 elders have? (See also Note 4:4 and Rev. 21:12–14).
- ❏ What does the scene around the throne include? Note its many OT images (Gen. 9:12–17; Ex. 19:16–19; 25:31–40; 2 Chron. 4:2–6; Ezek. 1).
- ❏ What about the four living creatures suggests the eternal power of God? (See Note 4:6, 4:7). What response does the central figure elicit? Why?
- ❏ What does this say about who God is and how he relates to his creation?
- ❏ What aspect of creation best demonstrates God's glory and power to you? Why?
- ❏ How do you feel about the way you worship God? How can this vision of God enhance your worship life? Your everyday life?

TO CLOSE AND PRAY / 15–30 Minutes

- ❏ On a scale of 1 to 10, what number will describe your spiritual life this past week? Where are you struggling?
- ❏ What has given you reason to celebrate?
- ❏ How can this group pray for you in the coming week?

ᵃ5 Or *the sevenfold Spirit*

Notes

4:1–11 The first vision (1:9–3:22) was of the exalted Christ caring for the first-century church ("what is now"—1:19). In the second vision (4:1–16:21) "what will take place" (1:19; 4:1) in the future is revealed; i.e. the coming of God's kingdom. This will be a vision of "the terrible conflict that takes place on earth between the church and the demonic powers embodied in an apostate civilization—Rome in the first century and Antichrist at the end—[which] are in reality expressions in historical form of a fearful conflict in the spiritual world between the Kingdom of God and the kingdom of Satan" (Ladd). The second vision has a number of parts to it, of which the first two parts (chapters 4 and 5) take place in the throne room of heaven and serve as an introduction to the rest of the vision. The vision begins in heaven with God, who rules the universe. It is important to remember (in the midst of the dark days of the end times) that the presence of Almighty God in heaven is the ultimate reality within which these coming events are being played out.

4:1 *After this I looked.* This is a phrase which usually signals the start of a new division of the narrative. *a door.* Unlike the door into the kingdom (3:8) and the door into the heart (3:20), this is a door into heaven through which John is invited to pass ("Come up here") and so encounter the next part of his vision.

4:2 *a throne in heaven with someone sitting on it.* John is granted a vision of God on his throne. John does not so much describe the person or throne; instead he conveys a set of images that seek to capture in words what is surely beyond words. The image of the throne pervades Revelation, occurring more than 40 times.

4:3 What John saw was akin to the luminous sparkling of precious stones. Light was a common image by which God was described (e.g., Ps. 104:2; 1 Tim. 6:16). *jasper.* What is called jasper today is opaque, while this heavenly gem is described in 21:11 as a transparent crystal. *carnelian.* A fiery red mineral found in Sardis. *rainbow.* There is an arc of a rainbow around the throne the color of emerald green (unlike a normal rainbow which contains the full spectrum of colors). It is probably better to see these as symbols which seek to convey God arrayed in "unapproachable light whom no one has seen or can see" (1 Tim. 6:16).

4:4 *twenty-four elders.* There are various interpretations of these figures. Some say they represent the 24 orders of the church of the Old and New Testament (with the 12 patriarchs and the 12 apostles). Others hold that they are angels who assist in the ruling of the universe. In any case, they function to worship and serve God.

4:5 In the OT, the presence of God was frequently accompanied by thunder and lightning (Ex. 19:16–17; Job 37:2–5; Ps. 18:13–15; Ezek. 1:13), phenomena which give a sense of his awesome power. *seven lamps.* Probably a symbol of the presence of the Holy Spirit (see Note for 1:4).

4:6 *a sea of glass.* "We are intended to understand it as a visual phenomenon which adds to the awesome splendor of the throne room scene. Its crystal surface stretches out before the throne, reflecting the flashing, many-colored light from the throne ... " (Mounce). (For OT parallels to this image see Ex. 24:10; Ezek. 1:22). *four living creatures.* These are similar to the creatures ("seraphim," "cherubim") seen in the vision of Isaiah (Isa. 6:1–3) and Ezekiel (Ezek. 10:14). They are some sort of angelic order which serves God.

4:7 Their forms suggest "different aspects of nature: the wild beasts, domesticated animals, human beings and flying creatures" (Ladd). This in turn suggests that they may function to express God's will in all of creation. "Hendriksen interprets them as having the strength of a lion (Ps. 103:20), the ability to serve of an ox (cf. Heb. 1:14), the intelligence of a man (cf. Luke 15:10), and the swiftness (to serve) of an eagle (cf. Dan. 9:21)" (Mounce).

4:8 *wings.* This suggests that they are capable of rapid movement. *eyes.* This suggests that they are constantly watching what is happening. They are alert and knowledgeable. *Almighty.* The church, which is about to enter a time of persecution, needs to be reminded that God is a God of all power who will see them through their troubles.

UNIT 6—The Scroll and the Lamb / Revelation 5:1–14

Scripture

The Scroll and the Lamb

5 *Then I saw in the right hand of him who sat on the throne a scroll with writing on both sides and sealed with seven seals. ²And I saw a mighty angel proclaiming in a loud voice, "Who is worthy to break the seals and open the scroll?" ³But no one in heaven or on earth or under the earth could open the scroll or even look inside it. ⁴I wept and wept because no one was found who was worthy to open the scroll or look inside. ⁵Then one of the elders said to me, "Do not weep! See, the Lion of the tribe of Judah, the Root of David, has triumphed. He is able to open the scroll and its seven seals."*

⁶Then I saw a Lamb, looking as if it had been slain, standing in the center of the throne, encircled by the four living creatures and the elders. He had seven horns and seven eyes, which are the seven spirits of God sent out into all the earth. ⁷He came and took the scroll from the right hand of him who sat on the throne. ⁸And when he had taken it, the four living creatures and the twenty-four elders fell down before the Lamb. Each one had a harp and they were holding golden bowls full of incense, which are the prayers of the saints. ⁹And they sang a new song:

> *"You are worthy to take the scroll*
> *and to open its seals,*
> *because you were slain,*
> *and with your blood you purchased*
> *men for God*
> *from every tribe and language and*
> *people and nation.*
> *¹⁰You have made them to be a kingdom*
> *and priests to*
> *serve our God,*
> *and they will reign on the earth."*

¹¹Then I looked and heard the voice of many angels, numbering thousands upon thousands, and ten thousand times ten thousand. They encircled the throne and the living creatures and the elders. ¹²In a loud voice they sang:

> *"Worthy is the Lamb, who was slain, to receive power and wealth and wisdom and strength and honor and glory and praise!"*

¹³Then I heard every creature in heaven and on earth and under the earth and on the sea, and all that is in them, singing:

> *"To him who sits on the throne and to the Lamb be praise and honor and glory and power, for ever and ever!"*

¹⁴The four living creatures said, "Amen," and the elders fell down and worshiped.

Group Questions

TO BEGIN / 15 Minutes (Choose 1 or 2)

- ❏ What was the best choir or musical group you have ever heard (or participated in)?
- ❏ Around the house, are you more like a lion or a lamb? Why?

READ SCRIPTURE AND DISCUSS / 30 Minutes

- ❏ What do you think makes the scroll so significant? What dilemma does the sealed scroll pose?
- ❏ Why is Christ the only one worthy enough to open it (vv. 4,9; see John 1:29)? What titles are used to describe him? What does it mean that he is both a lion and a lamb? What does this mean for your life?
- ❏ What is the meaning of the seven horns and seven eyes (see Note 5:1 and 5:6)?
- ❏ Where does Christ appear? What is the significance of this? What is the response when he takes the scroll?
- ❏ Analyze the three songs: How is the Lamb described? Who comprises the first musical group? The second? The third? Who are the true kings and priests on earth?
- ❏ What would this vision and the one in chapter 4 have meant to the persecuted Christians of Asia? What do these visions say to us in the twentieth century as we view our out-of-control world? How does that change your perspective on life this week?

TO CLOSE AND PRAY / 15–30 Minutes

- ❏ What has been the climate in your spiritual life this week? Hot and dry? Stormy and blowing? Unpredictable—different every day?
- ❏ How can this group encourage your spiritual life?
- ❏ What prayer request do you want to share?

Notes

5:1–14 The scene moves from its focus on God and his surrounding attendants to the Lamb, who opens the sacred scroll and so initiates the final conflict with Satan and his forces.

5:1 *the right hand of him who sat on the throne.* It is God who holds the whole of human history in his hand. He is sovereign and no matter how strong evil may appear to be, it is he who controls the ultimate flow of events. *a scroll.* The nature of this scroll is not clear. The best guess is that this scroll is like the one given to Ezekiel, containing "words of lament and mourning and woe" (Ezek. 2:10). In this case, John's scroll would contain "the prophecy of the end events, including both the salvation of God's people and the judgment of the wicked" (Ladd). *seven.* The number seven occurs frequently in Revelation, as indeed it does in the rest of the Bible. It has to do with completeness; it relates to the fullness of something. God created the earth in six days and rested on the seventh. As the world began in seven days, so it will end by a series of sevens. *seals.* The scroll is rolled up and sealed along its edge with seven wax seals (that ensure the secrecy of its contents), which must be broken in order for the contents to be read. As each seal is broken, a momentous event takes place.

5:2–3 The call goes out across creation ("in heaven or on earth or under the earth") for someone to bring history to its conclusion, but no one is found.

5:4 So overwhelming is the thought that God's final action in history has to be postponed for want of a worthy mediator that John bursts into tears.

5:5 The elder calms John. There is one who is worthy to perform this task. It is Christ who can and will reveal where history is going and how it will end. The meaning of history (which is contained in the scroll) cannot be known apart from Christ. *the Lion of the tribe of Judah.* An ancient title for the Messiah (Gen. 49:9–10) which was in use in the first century. The image is of a conquering King. *the Root of David.* Another messianic title, referring this time to the fact that the Messiah will come from the royal family of David (Isa. 11:1). *triumphed.* By his death on the cross, Jesus won a great victory over evil, sin, and death (Col. 2:15; 2 Tim. 1:10; Heb. 2:14–15). Though this victory is real and eternal, its full realization will occur only at the end of time. This assertion functions to confirm once more that despite the great battles that lie ahead, the outcome is certain.

5:6 *a Lamb.* The Lion has become a Lamb. The final victory of the conquering Messiah is only possible because of the death of the Lamb of God. In the OT a lamb was sacrificed each Passover, reminding the nation that God had spared them and delivered them from the bondage of Egypt (Ex. 12:13). Interestingly, the connection was not made between the slain lamb and the Messiah prior to NT revelation, despite the prophecy in Isaiah 53. Until Jesus, people could not conceive of a conquering Messiah who was slain as a sacrificial lamb. *seven horns.* A horn is a symbol of power in the OT (e.g., Deut. 33:17; Ps. 18:2). Seven horns would represent the fullness of power (see Matt. 28:18). *seven eyes.* He also has fullness of vision, i.e., omniscience (see Zech. 4:10).

5:8 When the Lamb grasps the scroll of history, the whole of heaven bursts into a song of praise. *incense.* Incense was used in OT worship (Deut. 33:10). Here it stands for the prayers of God's people.

5:9 *a new song.* A special song composed for this momentous occasion when a whole new order of reality is about to be instituted. *purchased.* Ransomed—a word used to describe the freeing of a slave from bondage by the payment of a price. The purchase price, in this case, was the blood of Christ. What it bought was the freedom of men and women from the bondage of sin. *from every tribe and language and people and nation.* Christ redeems people from the whole of humankind—past, present, and future—by this great and terrible payment.

5:10 *a kingdom and priests.* The result is that they have become God's people and God's priests. They will share in God's rule and they will have access to his presence. *reign on earth.* In order for his people to reign on earth, his kingdom must be established there in fullness; and thus it is necessary to break the seals and so bring about the kingdom.

UNIT 7—The Seals / Revelation 6:1–17

Scripture

The Seals

6 I watched as the Lamb opened the first of the seven seals. Then I heard one of the four living creatures say in a voice like thunder, "Come!" [2]I looked, and there before me was a white horse! Its rider held a bow, and he was given a crown, and he rode out as a conqueror bent on conquest.

[3]When the Lamb opened the second seal, I heard the second living creature say, "Come!" [4]Then another horse came out, a fiery red one. Its rider was given power to take peace from the earth and to make men slay each other. To him was given a large sword.

[5]When the Lamb opened the third seal, I heard the third living creature say, "Come!" I looked, and there before me was a black horse! Its rider was holding a pair of scales in his hand. [6]Then I heard what sounded like a voice among the four living creatures, saying, "A quart of wheat for a day's wages, and three quarts of barley for a day's wages, and do not damage the oil and the wine!"

[7]When the Lamb opened the fourth seal, I heard the voice of the fourth living creature say, "Come!" [8]I looked, and there before me was a pale horse! Its rider was named Death, and Hades was following close behind him. They were given power over a fourth of the earth to kill by sword, famine and plague, and by the wild beasts of the earth.

[9]When he opened the fifth seal, I saw under the altar the souls of those who had been slain because of the word of God and the testimony they had maintained. [10]They called out in a loud voice, "How long, Sovereign Lord, holy and true, until you judge the inhabitants of the earth and avenge our blood?" [11]Then each of them was given a white robe, and they were told to wait a little longer, until the number of their fellow servants and brothers who were to be killed as they had been was completed.

[12]I watched as he opened the sixth seal. There was a great earthquake. The sun turned black like sackcloth made of goat hair, the whole moon turned blood red, [13]and the stars in the sky fell to earth, as late figs drop from a fig tree when shaken by a strong wind. [14]The sky receded like a scroll, rolling up, and every mountain and island was removed from its place.

[15]Then the kings of the earth, the princes, the generals, the rich, the mighty, and every slave and every free man hid in caves and among the rocks of the mountains. [16]They called to the mountains and the rocks, "Fall on us and hide us from the face of him who sits on the throne and from the wrath of the Lamb! [17]For the great day of their wrath has come, and who can stand?"

Group Questions

TO BEGIN / 15 Minutes (Choose 1 or 2)

❑ What is your favorite kind of horse?
❑ Who is the best horseman in your family?

READ SCRIPTURE AND DISCUSS / 30 Minutes

❑ How do these events relate to the Great Tribulation?
❑ Who (or what) do each of the four horsemen represent? (See Notes.) How are the first two horsemen similar? How are they different?
❑ When the third horseman rides, how much food will a day's wages buy? Why will luxury items (wine and oil) still be available? What is the relationship of this to the first two horsemen? In what sense do they lead to the fourth horseman?
❑ How have each of these forces operated throughout history? How do they prevail today? What do you think this means for the interpretation of the vision?
❑ What is revealed by the opening of the fifth seal? How is this related to the suffering of the Christians in John's day? In our day?
❑ What occurs when the sixth seal is broken (see Mark 13)?
❑ Who can stand under the wrath of God? How?
❑ How does this passage make you feel about the end times? Why? How will this affect your actions this week?

TO CLOSE AND PRAY / 15–30 Minutes

❑ If you were to write a letter about your spiritual life this past week would it be full of good news or struggles?
❑ What might God's letter to you be saying this week?
❑ What prayer requests would you like to share?

Notes

6:1–8:1 The vision in the throne room of heaven (chapters 4–5) sets the stage for the unfolding judgment of the second vision (chapters 6–16) beginning here with the opening of the seven seals (6:1–8:1). The seven seals must be broken before the contents of the scroll can be read. What is contained here is not the Great Tribulation, but those events which precede it.

6:1–2 The first seal is broken by the Lamb himself, the only one worthy to set in motion these momentous events. *a white horse.* There has been much debate about the identity of the rider on the white horse. One suggestion is that he symbolizes military conquest, an image in line with the identity of the other three riders. Another suggestion is that the rider on a white horse symbolizes the preaching of the Gospel throughout the world prior to the end. The bow is used in the OT as a symbol of divine victories (Hab. 3:9). In Revelation, white is generally a symbol of Christ (e.g., 1:14; 14:14; 19:11,14). Furthermore, unlike the coming of the other three horsemen, no calamities follow after this rider.

6:3–4 The second seal is broken and a red horse and rider appear. There is no ambiguity about this figure: it is a symbol of bloodshed and war. "If the first seal suggested invasion from without, the second seal may refer to internal strife. ... His mission is to remove peace from the earth and allow men to turn their destructive instincts upon one another" (Mounce).

6:5 The third seal is broken and a black horse and rider are called forth, symbolizing a time of great scarcity verging on famine.

6:6 Food is sold at inflated prices—over 10 times what it should cost. *a day's wages.* In those days, a man earned a denarius (a Roman coin) for a day's work (Matt. 20:2). This was normally enough to feed a whole family, but now it could only buy enough wheat (the staple food of the area) for a single person.

6:7–8 The fourth horse and rider represent death from various causes. These are the "four dreadful judgments" in Ezekiel 14:21. *Hades.* After death comes the grave or the underworld. Hades was understood to be the place where the dead dwelt. *famine.* The issue is no longer scarcity (as with the black horse), but a severe lack of food that leads to death.

6:9 A new scene unfolds with the breaking of the fifth seal. Those who have been martyred in the name of God are pictured under the altar. "That the souls of the martyrs were underneath the altar is a way of saying that their untimely deaths on earth are from God's perspective a sacrifice on the altar of heaven" (Mounce). *the testimony they had maintained.* This probably refers not to testimony as "witnessing" to others about their faith, but rather to the fact that they had maintained even unto death their faithfulness to the witness Jesus had given; i.e., they remained loyal to the Gospel.

6:10 *holy.* The martyrs appeal to his holiness. He is beyond all evil and so can be relied upon to right the wrong done to them. *the inhabitants of the earth.* In Revelation, this phrase refers to those who are hostile to God.

6:12–14 The sixth seal is broken and John sees cosmic disturbances which herald the coming of the last days. This is pictorial language not intended to be taken literally, but which, nevertheless, describes a real catastrophe of cosmic proportions. *sun/moon/stars.* Even the predictable, well-ordered movement of the heavenly bodies goes awry (see Isa. 34:4; Acts 2:20). *receded like a scroll.* The image is of a papyrus scroll stretched out across the sky which snaps in the middle and rolls up quickly on either side.

6:15–17 This is a terror so great that it drives men and women of all classes to seek cover from the wrath of the one who is bringing about the end (Isa. 2:19; Mal. 3:2). *the wrath of the Lamb.* An unusual phrase, since a lamb is thought of as gentle— "a deliberate paradox, by which John intends to goad his readers into theological alertness" (Caird). *the great day of their wrath.* There are many titles used to describe this period of time. In this case the focus is on judgment; on the fact that those who have rebelled against God will face his judgment. So terrifying is this that "better death by a crushing avalanche than face the wrath of the Lamb ..." (Mounce).

UNIT 8—144,000 Sealed / The Great Multitude in White Robes / Revelation 7:1–17

Scripture

144,000 Sealed

7 *After this I saw four angels standing at the four corners of the earth, holding back the four winds of the earth to prevent any wind from blowing on the land or on the sea or on any tree. ²Then I saw another angel coming up from the east, having the seal of the living God. He called out in a loud voice to the four angels who had been given power to harm the land and the sea: ³"Do not harm the land or the sea or the trees until we put a seal on the foreheads of the servants of our God." ⁴Then I heard the number of those who were sealed: 144,000 from all the tribes of Israel.*

⁵From the tribe of Judah 12,000 were sealed,
from the tribe of Reuben 12,000,
from the tribe of Gad 12,000,
⁶from the tribe of Asher 12,000,
from the tribe of Naphtali 12,000,
from the tribe of Manasseh 12,000,
⁷from the tribe of Simeon 12,000,
from the tribe of Levi 12,000,
from the tribe of Issachar 12,000,
⁸from the tribe of Zebulun 12,000,
from the tribe of Joseph 12,000,
from the tribe of Benjamin 12,000.

The Great Multitude in White Robes

⁹After this I looked and there before me was a great multitude that no one could count, from every nation, tribe, people and language, standing before the throne and in front of the Lamb. They were wearing white robes and were holding palm branches in their hands. ¹⁰And they cried out in a loud voice:

"Salvation belongs to our God,
who sits on the throne,
and to the Lamb."

Group Questions

TO BEGIN / 15 Minutes (Choose 1 or 2)

❏ Who in your family likes to study about the end times?
❏ What is the windiest place where you have ever lived or visited?

READ SCRIPTURE AND DISCUSS / 15–30 Minutes

❏ Do you think the work of the four angels is a "new" woe, or is it a restatement of the events in chapter 6? Why? Likewise, in what sense do the events in chapter 7 come "after" the events in chapter 6: In actual history? Or simply in John's vision?
❏ What is the message of the fifth angel? Who is sealed? When does this occur? What does it mean (see Gen. 4:15; Ezek. 9:4–6; Eph. 1:13–14)?
❏ Is this "144,000" a symbol or a statistic? Why (see 7:9; 14:1–5)? How have you sensed God's protection in the last six months? Before that?
❏ What sort of seal has God placed on your life? How is this seal evident to other Christians? To non-Christians? Why?
❏ In verses 9–17, what does John see next? How does he describe the size of the crowd? Is this multitude the same as the 144,000 (v. 4)? Why or why not? What are they doing? Wearing? Carrying?
❏ What's the significance of the white robes, the palm branches and the washing? What is the new function of those in white robes? What is their future? How would this encourage the Christians of John's day? Of our day?
❏ When the multitude cries out, how do the angels, elders, and the four living creatures respond? What does all this say about God's kingdom and Christ's sacrifice?
❏ What qualifies this white-robed crowd to stand before God? What is their new role? What is "the Great Tribulation"—is it a particular event or a general experience?
❏ Is the safety, security and service of these Christians a present life experience for them, or only a promise to be realized in some vague and distant future? Or both?

[Scripture and Group Questions continued on page 30]

Notes

7:1–17 Chapter 7 is a dramatic interlude between the opening of the sixth and the seventh seal, in which the security of the faithful is set in contrast to the panic of the world. It consists of two parts: the sealing of the 144,000 (7:1–8) and the blessedness of the great multitude before the throne (7:9–17). Interludes are used by John at several points in his account (e.g., 10:1–11:13). They provide background information for the narrative which follows. In this case, just prior to the Great Tribulation, the church needs to know that it will survive this ordeal. Chapter 7 answers the question posed in 6:17: "Who can stand?"

7:1–4 The earth is pictured as a great square, with an angel at each corner holding back a lethal wind until the 144,000 can be sealed. *a seal.* Probably similar to the signet ring which kings used to authenticate documents by its imprint. The purpose of this seal is to mark out God's people so that they will be spared from the plagues that are to come (9:4). This is similar to the time of the Exodus, when the tenth plague brought death to the firstborn of those households not marked by blood over the door. "God will protect his people from the outpouring of his wrath even though they must suffer tribulation at the hands of the Antichrist" (Ladd).

7:5–8 The process of sealing is not discussed further. John simply lists the 12 tribes of Israel, from each of which 12,000 are sealed. There has been great discussion among scholars as to who these 144,000 might be. Some say they are representatives of the Jewish people and point to the salvation of (literal) Israel. Others say that the 144,000 represent converted Israel. Still others say that they represent spiritual Israel, i.e., the church. Wilcock contends, rightly it seems, that "the servants of God, all of them, Old Testament and New, all his believing people, are sealed." The interpretation of the 144,000 as "spiritual Israel" arises from the fact that the 12 tribes listed in these verses do not correspond to any of the 18 lists of the 12 tribes in the OT (see, for example, Gen. 49 and Ezek. 48). The most obvious problem with this list is that the tribe of Dan is omitted. The tribe of Ephraim is also omitted, but it is referred to in an indirect way by the mention of Joseph who was the father of Ephraim (as well as Manasseh, who is mentioned in the list). "No satisfactory explanation of this irregular list of names has

been offered, unless it be this: John intends to say that the 12 tribes of Israel are not really literal Israel, but the true, spiritual Israel—the church" (Ladd). This accords with the NT view of the church as the new Israel (see Rom. 2:28–29; 4:11; Gal. 3:29; Phil. 3:3; Rev. 2:9; 3:9). If this is what is intended (and this is the view taken in these notes), then chapter seven provides two glimpses of the church. First, it is seen prior to the Tribulation, being prepared to go through this awful time (7:1–7) and then, second, it is shown victorious after the Tribulation (7:8–17). *12,000.* This number is symbolic, as is the total number of 144,000 (12 squared times a thousand) and conveys the idea of completeness: 12,000 are sealed from each of the 12 tribes. The full complement is sealed.

7:5 Judah heads the list, not Reuben, who belongs in that place as Jacob's oldest son (Gen. 49:3). Probably the reason for this is that Christ came from the tribe of Judah ("the lion of the tribe of Judah"—see 5:5).

7:9–17 The focus now shifts from before the Tribulation to after it. A multitude stands before God, consisting of people from across the planet. John's view has moved beyond the dark time of the Tribulation to the final victory which will be the ultimate reality.

7:10 The song they sing is not, as one might expect, one of gratitude to God for their deliverance. Rather, it is a song of praise to God for his work of salvation. Their salvation involves more than just deliverance from the Tribulation.

7:11–12 The heavenly beings—the angels, the elders, and the four living creatures—chime in with their own song: a seven-fold doxology of praise in which they heap up, one upon another, God's attributes. *glory.* A reference to the brightness of God, his divine luminous presence. *thanks.* For his great work of salvation by which he has overcome evil and established his kingdom. *honor.* The greatness of his work is acknowledged publicly. *power.* The fact that when God acts, he cannot be overcome. *might.* "His redemptive presence in the events of history" (Mounce).

7:13–14 The question of the identity of the great multitude is raised and then answered. This question

[Notes continued on page 31]

Scripture (Continued)

*[11]All the angels were standing around the
throne and around the elders and the four living creatures. They fell down on their faces
before the throne and worshiped God, [12]say-
ing:*

> *"Amen!*
> *Praise and glory*
> *and wisdom and thanks and honor*
> *and power and strength*
> *be to our God for ever and ever.*
> *Amen!"*

*[13]Then one of the elders asked me, "These
in white robes—who are they, and where did
they come from?"*
[14]I answered, "Sir, you know."
*And he said, "These are they who have
come out of the great tribulation; they have
washed their robes and made them white in
the blood of the Lamb. [15]Therefore,*

> *"they are before the throne of God*
> *and serve him day and night in his temple;*
> *and he who sits on the throne will spread*
> *his tent over them.*
> *[16]Never again will they hunger;*
> *never again will they thirst.*
> *The sun will not beat upon them,*
> *nor any scorching heat.*
> *[17]For the Lamb at the center of the throne*
> *will be their shepherd;*
> *he will lead them to springs of living*
> *water.*
> *And God will wipe away every tear from*
> *their eyes."*

Group Questions (Continued)

❑ What is your greatest tribulation or persecution?
How difficult does it seem next to that faced by the
people of John's day? Why? How difficult does it
seem next to the majesty of God seen in this passage? Why? How will you incorporate this into your
life?

TO CLOSE AND PRAY / 15–30 Minutes

❑ In what area of your life do you need a fresh wind
from God? Why?
❑ How has this group been a fresh wind in your life?
❑ What would you like this group to pray about for you
this week?

Notes (Continued)

and answer process is often used in prophetic literature when a vision is to be explained (see Jer. 1:11,13; 24:3; Amos 7:8; 8:2; Zech. 4:5).

7:14 they who have come out of. In the narrow sense, these are the martyrs from the Great Tribulation: those who maintained their faith to the point of death. But "the larger context favors a point in time when the complete number of the redeemed stand before God and the blessings of the eternal state are about to be realized" (Mounce). **the great tribulation.** This event is mentioned in both the Old and New Testament. Daniel 12:1 refers to the "time of distress" (literally, "tribulation" in Greek) that will come. Jesus picks up these words of Daniel and expands upon them: "For then there will be great distress, unequaled from the beginning of the world until now—and never to be equaled again. If those days had not been cut short, no one would survive, but for the sake of the elect those days will be shortened" (Matt. 24:21–22). Though suffering has been the lot of God's people down through the ages (John 16:33; 2 Tim. 3:12), this will be a time of unparalleled persecution and conflict.

7:15 spread his tent over them. A reference to the tabernacle in the wilderness (Lev. 26:11–13) where God's presence dwelt. That his tent is over them would mean that they are now drawn into his presence, rather than standing outside the tent. This is "a way of saying that the immediate presence of God will shelter and protect them from all that would harm (Isa. 4:5–6)" (Mounce). See also Ezekiel 37:27; Zechariah 2:10.

7:16–17 The experience described here sounds like the experience of the kingdom of God come in its completeness, since the language parallels the discussion of that reality in 21:1–5 and 22:1–5.

7:16 never again will they hunger/thirst. Such a promise was especially significant to people of that era who knew famine and where, in many regions, water was scarce. This promise, however, goes beyond physical provision. The satisfying of hunger and thirst is used in Scripture as a metaphor for spiritual satisfaction (Matt. 5:6; John 6:35). **sun/scorching heat.** Again, to people living in the Middle East, the promise of shelter from the intensity of the sun was welcome indeed. Again, this has spiritual implications. "They are sheltered from all discomfort by the presence of God" (Mounce).

7:17 the Lamb ... will be their shepherd. A curious image: the Lamb becomes the shepherd (who tends the flock of lambs). However, with the fluid language of visions, it is appropriate that both these descriptions of the Messiah be expressed. In the OT, God is frequently portrayed as the shepherd of his people; i.e., the one who gives guidance, provides for needs, and protects his flock (see Ps. 23:1; Isa. 40:11; Ezek. 34:23). In the NT Jesus is pictured as the Good Shepherd (John 10:1–30; 21:15–17). **he will lead them to springs of living water.** His main role here, however, is to lead the flock to the water of life which is the presence of God (see John 4:14). **wipe away every tear.** Their suffering is now past. There is a new reality in which tears are not necessary. Joy will be their portion. (See 21:4.)

31

UNIT 9—The Seventh Seal/The Trumpets / Rev. 8:1–13

Scripture

The Seventh Seal and the Golden Censer

8 *When he opened the seventh seal, there was silence in heaven for about half an hour.*

²And I saw the seven angels who stand before God, and to them were given seven trumpets.

³Another angel, who had a golden censer, came and stood at the altar. He was given much incense to offer, with the prayers of all the saints, on the golden altar before the throne. ⁴The smoke of the incense, together with the prayers of the saints, went up before God from the angel's hand. ⁵Then the angel took the censer, filled it with fire from the altar, and hurled it on the earth; and there came peals of thunder, rumblings, flashes of lightning and an earthquake.

The Trumpets

⁶Then the seven angels who had the seven trumpets prepared to sound them.

⁷The first angel sounded his trumpet, and there came hail and fire mixed with blood, and it was hurled down upon the earth. A third of the earth was burned up, a third of the trees were burned up, and all the green grass was burned up.

⁸The second angel sounded his trumpet, and something like a huge mountain, all ablaze, was thrown into the sea. A third of the sea turned into blood, ⁹a third of the living creatures in the sea died, and a third of the ships were destroyed.

¹⁰The third angel sounded his trumpet, and a great star, blazing like a torch, fell from the sky on a third of the rivers and on the springs of water—¹¹the name of the star is Wormwood.ᵃ A third of the waters turned bitter, and many people died from the waters that had become bitter.

¹²The fourth angel sounded his trumpet, and a third of the sun was struck, a third of the moon, and a third of the stars, so that a third of them turned dark. A third of the day was without light, and also a third of the night.

¹³As I watched, I heard an eagle that was flying in midair call out in a loud voice:

"Woe! Woe! Woe to the inhabitants of the earth, because of the trumpet blasts about to be sounded by the other three angels!"

ᵃ11 That is, Bitterness

Group Questions

TO BEGIN / 15 Minutes (Choose 1 or 2)

- ❏ When home alone, do you like silence, or do you have to have some noise going on? Why?
- ❏ When you're working and want to listen to background music, what kind do you choose?

READ SCRIPTURE AND DISCUSS / 30 Minutes

- ❏ Amid seals and trumpets, why this silence? When have you tried silent meditation or contemplative prayer?
- ❏ What is a censer? What do altars and incense teach about prayer (vv. 3–5, see 5:8; 6:9–10; 9:13)? When was the last time you cried for justice or mercy?
- ❏ What events follow the sounding of each of the first four trumpets? What do the trumpets signify: Triumph or doom? Life or death? What else?
- ❏ How do these trumpeted events compare with the events inaugurated by the first six seals?
- ❏ Likewise, how do these events compare with the plagues in Exodus 7–10 and Joel 2:1–11?
- ❏ What parallels or repeated patterns do you see between the opening of the seals and the sounding of the trumpets? Which suggests that these two scenes are in reality two sides of the same coin? (Note how the trumpets focus on what will happen to the unbelieving world, whereas the seals focus on what will happen to the church.)
- ❏ Do these seals and trumpets refer to datable and sequential events, or to aspects of the world condition (which may be true at any point in history)? Why?
- ❏ How has the star named "Wormwood" (v. 11) or "Bitterness" affected your life? How has your bitterness affected others? What have you discovered as an antidote to bitterness?

TO CLOSE AND PRAY / 15–30 Minutes

- ❏ What issue in your life has needed quiet prayer this week but you never got around to it?
- ❏ How can this group pray for you this week?

Notes

8:1–9:21 The breaking of the first six seals (ch. 6) revealed what would happen in the troubled times just prior to the end. At the breaking of the sixth seal, the end was announced via cosmic disturbances. Before details of the end times are given, however, there was an interlude (ch. 7) in which the fate of the church is revealed. Chapters 8 and 9 then recount the breaking of the final seal and the sounding of the first six trumpets.

8:1 The breaking of the seventh seal opens the scroll so that the events of the end times can be revealed. "The first six seals, representing events preliminary to the end or the 'beginning of woes' (Matt. 24:8), have now been broken and the time has come for the breaking of the final seal, the opening of the book, and the story of the end itself" (Ladd). *the seventh seal.* Unlike the other seals (with the possible exception of the first seal), the breaking of this seal brings no judgment. There is silence while the seven angels prepare to sound the seven trumpets, and the other angel mingles the incense and the prayers of the saints and then flings the censer to earth. It would appear that the seven trumpets are the contents of the seventh seal. *silence.* The nature of this silence is not clear. Some say it represents the beginning of eternal rest for the multitudes, but this is out of character with the other seals. Others suggest that it is the time when the prayers of the saints are heard (vv. 3–4). Probably the silence is meant to indicate a moment of suspense before the events of the trumpets unfold.

8:2 *the seven angels.* Who they are is not defined, though they appear to be a specific group of heavenly beings. *trumpets.* In the OT, trumpets are used for various purposes: to signal various activities (Num. 10:1–10); as part of worship and celebration (Num. 10:10; 29:1); in war (Josh. 6); and at coronations (1 Kings 1:34). Here in Revelation, however, they have the more ominous purpose of announcing and loosing eschatological plagues.

8:3-5 There is a short period of preparation before the sounding of the first trumpet. "The vision of the angel casting a censer on the altar conveys the simple truth, already expressed in the prayer of the souls of the martyrs under the altar (6:9–11), that God's judgments will come upon the world in answer to the prayers of the saints" (Ladd).

8:7 The second series of calamities begins. "While the first four seals depicted judgments which are the inevitable consequences of human sinfulness, the trumpets reveal the active involvement of God in bringing punishment upon a wicked world" (Mounce). As will become evident, the aim of these acts of judgment is to lead people to repentance (see 9:20; 16:10). *a third of the earth burned up.* The first plague destroys a third of the earth's vegetation. This is similar to the seventh Egyptian plague (Ex. 9:13–35). *fire.* The fire that is mixed with hail may be lightning. *blood.* Probably a reference to the color of the storm, not the destruction it caused.

8:8–9 The second plague is unique; it is impossible to parallel it with any known natural event (e.g., a volcano). It destroys a third of the sea, along with a third of the fish under the sea and a third of the boats on top of the sea. This plague is similar to what happened to the Nile in Exodus 7:20–21.

8:10–11 During the third plague, a great meteor falls from the sky and poisons a third of the fresh water. *Wormwood.* A plant which has a bitter taste.

8:12 The fourth plague strikes the heavenly bodies. A third of the sun, moon and stars go dark. This is similar to the ninth plague in Egypt (Ex. 10:21–23). *without light.* It was not just that the intensity of the light was reduced by a third; there was absolute darkness for a third of the time.

8:13 The first four trumpets have been sounded and four plagues have fallen upon the earth. Prior to the next two plagues (which will fall upon human beings), a warning is sounded. *Woe!* The triple "Woe" corresponds to the final three trumpets (see 9:12). *the inhabitants of the earth.* These plagues will come upon those who are hostile to God (see note for 6:10). Somehow the church—those who have God's seal upon them—will be spared (see 9:4).

UNIT 10—The Trumpets, continued / Rev. 9:1–21

Scripture

9 The fifth angel sounded his trumpet, and I saw a star that had fallen from the sky to the earth. The star was given the key to the shaft of the Abyss. ²When he opened the Abyss, smoke rose from it like the smoke from a gigantic furnace. The sun and sky were darkened by the smoke from the Abyss. ³And out of the smoke locusts came down upon the earth and were given power like that of scorpions of the earth. ⁴They were told not to harm the grass of the earth or any plant or tree, but only those people who did not have the seal of God on their foreheads. ⁵They were not given power to kill them, but only to torture them for five months. And the agony they suffered was like that of the sting of a scorpion when it strikes a man. ⁶During those days men will seek death, but will not find it; they will long to die, but death will elude them.

⁷The locusts looked like horses prepared for battle. On their heads they wore something like crowns of gold, and their faces resembled human faces. ⁸Their hair was like women's hair, and their teeth were like lions' teeth. ⁹They had breastplates like breastplates of iron, and the sound of their wings was like the thundering of many horses and chariots rushing into battle. ¹⁰They had tails and stings like scorpions, and in their tails they had power to torment people for five months. ¹¹They had as king over them the angel of the Abyss, whose name in Hebrew is Abaddon, and in Greek, Apollyon.ᵃ

¹²The first woe is past; two other woes are yet to come.

¹³The sixth angel sounded his trumpet, and I heard a voice coming from the hornsᵇ of the golden altar that is before God. ¹⁴It said to the sixth angel who had the trumpet, "Release the four angels who are bound at the great river Euphrates." ¹⁵And the four angels who had been kept ready for this very hour and day and month and year were released to kill a

[Scripture continued on page 36]

ᵃ11 *Abaddon* and *Apollyon* mean *Destroyer.*   ᵇ13 That is, *projections*

Group Questions

TO BEGIN / 15 Minutes (Choose 1 or 2)

❏ What is one of the most excruciating pains you've ever experienced? What happened?
❏ When do you still dream about a scary or painful experience? What happened?

READ SCRIPTURE AND DISCUSS / 30 Minutes

❏ What happens when the fifth trumpet sounds? Who could the fallen star be (see Luke 10:18; Isa. 14:12)? What does "the Abyss" represent?
❏ What power do the locusts have? Describe them? What do they represent?
❏ Are the four angels in verse 14 good or evil? What is God's role in their actions?
❏ What is the difference between the power of the locusts and the power of the horses?
❏ What events are inaugurated by the sixth trumpet? What response should this woe elicit from the unbelieving world? Why? Why do you suppose this woe failed to bring the majority to repentance as originally intended?
❏ What do you think of Christians who pray for trouble to strike the unbelieving world? What do you think of God's answer to such prayers in this passage? By Christians today?
❏ What modern-day realities does the imagery of these plagues bring to mind for you? How might they have applied equally well in John's day?
❏ What do you see in our society that fits with the actions listed in verses 20 and 21? Which of these actions do you see in your own life? In what way? What can you do about this in the coming week?

TO CLOSE AND PRAY / 15–30 Minutes

❏ What color would you use to describe your past week? Why? Your past year? Why?
❏ What has "plagued" your life this week?
❏ How can this group support you in the challenges you are facing?
❏ How can this group pray for you this week?

Notes

9:1–12 The fifth plague (the first woe) is recounted in more detail than the first four. It involves the attack of fierce locusts who sting but do not kill. In Joel 2:1–11, it had been prophesied that a plague of locusts would precede the Day of the Lord.

9:1 *a star.* A heavenly figure with the power to unlock the underworld. *the Abyss.* In the pictorial way in which the Bible speaks of the cosmos, there are said to be three levels: the heavens, the earth, and the underworld (which is a huge, bottomless pit). It is the realm of the dead (Rom. 10:7); it is where the beast abides (Rev. 11:7); it is the place of demons (Luke 8:31); it will be used as the prison of Satan during the Millennium (Rev. 20:3); and in this case, it is the home of the demon locusts. The Abyss is connected to the surface of the earth via a shaft.

9:3 *locusts.* These are not actual locusts, but some sort of demonic entity. Their coming is similar to the plague of (real) locusts in Exodus 10:1–20. *scorpions.* A large spider-like poisonous creature which has a stinger on the end of its tail.

9:4 Real locusts consume plants, trees, and grass. These locusts lack that ability, attacking only human beings. *the seal of God.* (See 7:3.) God's wrath will not fall upon those who are his people; only upon those who worship the beast (16:2). This is not to say that God's people will be spared suffering and persecution—only that it will not be from God.

9:5 *five months.* The significance of this time period is not clear. It may refer to the life cycle of the locust (which is five months), or to the five-month period when an invasion of locusts is most likely. Probably it is merely intended to indicate that the suffering will be confined to a short period of time. The aim of these acts after all is not to torment but to bring about repentance.

9:7–10 The description of the locusts cannot be pressed too much beyond what John actually says. They are strange, weird creatures of hell with no true parallel in daily reality.

9:7 The locusts looked like horses. In some cultures (e.g., in Arabia), the head of the locust is thought to look like the head of a horse. In Joel 2:4, the locusts are described as war horses. *crowns.* These symbolize, perhaps, the fact that the locusts have the power to succeed in their mission to torment humankind. *human faces.* This may refer to their intelligence.

9:8 *hair like women's hair.* Perhaps a reference to the antennae of locusts, or to the hair on their legs or bodies. *lion's teeth.* Locusts are fierce in the way they destroy vegetation. This feature is mentioned in Joel 1:6.

9:9 *breastplates of iron.* The scales on the body of locusts are shaped like this. *the sound of their wings.* When locusts swarm into an area, they make a loud noise by the beating of their wings. This characteristic is mentioned in Joel 2:4–5.

9:11 *king over them.* This figure is unique with no parallel in biblical or other Jewish literature. *Abaddon.* A Hebrew word meaning "destruction." In the OT, this word is used along with Sheol for the place of destruction; the place of the dead (Job 26:6; 28:22; Prov. 15:11; 27:20). *Apollyon.* This Greek word is not the usual word used to translate *abaddon.* It is a participle meaning "destroyer." Many feel that this is a reference to the Greek god Apollo, one of whose symbols was the locust. The Roman emperor Domitian considered himself to be the incarnation of Apollo, so this might be a cryptic reference to the evil of the Roman emperors.

9:12 This refers back to 8:13. The first woe is passed. The second will be described in 9:13–21, when the sixth trumpet is sounded. The third woe will come when the seventh trumpet is sounded in 11:14. (The nature of the third woe is unclear, since the seventh trumpet [like the seventh seal] does not lead to a specific calamity but to a new scene. Some commentators feel that the third woe is the coming of Satan in 12:7–9, which is described as a woe in 12:12.)

9:13–21 The plague of the fifth trumpet brought pain and suffering; this plague brings death. The OT parallel for such an invasion of horses is found in Ezekiel 38:14–16 (see also Isa. 5:26–30; Jer. 6:22–26). Perhaps the historical image that lies behind this vision has to do with the Parthian horse-

[Notes continued on page 37]

Scripture

third of mankind. ¹⁶The number of the mounted troops was two hundred million. I heard their number.

¹⁷The horses and riders I saw in my vision looked like this: Their breastplates were fiery red, dark blue, and yellow as sulfur. The heads of the horses resembled the heads of lions, and out of their mouths came fire, smoke and sulfur. ¹⁸A third of mankind was killed by the three plagues of fire, smoke and sulfur that came out of their mouths. ¹⁹The power of the horses was in their mouths and in their tails; for their tails were like snakes, having heads with which they inflict injury.

²⁰The rest of mankind that were not killed by these plagues still did not repent of the work of their hands; they did not stop worshiping demons, and idols of gold, silver, bronze, stone and wood—idols that cannot see or hear or walk. ²¹Nor did they repent of their murders, their magic arts, their sexual immorality or their thefts.

Notes (Continued)

man who threatened the peace of Rome (see Note for 6:1–2).

9:13 *a voice coming from the horns of the golden altar.* This is the voice of the martyrs whose prayers are upon the throne, crying out for vindication (see 6:9–10; 8:3).

9:14 *the four angels.* Again, as with the seven trumpet-angels, this appears to be a definite group. However, four angels such as these are nowhere mentioned in apocalyptic literature. *bound.* These are probably fallen angels, held in check so they could not exercise their evil intentions. Now they are released and they kill a third of mankind. How this killing takes place is not indicated. Probably they were commanders of the great army of horses. *the great river Euphrates.* The eastern boundary of the Promised Land (Gen. 15:18). Beyond it lived the enemies of the Jewish nation. The releasing of these hordes would probably conjure up images for John's readers of the fearful Parthians.

9:15 The evil angels have no power to act until God allows it.

9:16 *two hundred million.* This is a number beyond imagination in those days. It would be a limitless horde to the readers.

9:17 *the horses.* The demon locusts in the previous plague are followed by demon horses in this plague.

There is a difference, however. While the locusts had the power to torture, the horses have the power to kill. *I saw in my vision.* These are not natural creatures; they are demon hordes revealed in an ecstatic vision. *their breastplates.* This description could refer to the armor of the riders or to the armor of both riders and horses. Beyond this, little is said about the riders. The focus is on the terrifying horses. *fire, smoke and sulfur.* Fire, smoke and sulfur (brimstone) of this sort are straight out of hell (14:10–11; 19:20; 21:8).

9:18 The fire, smoke and sulphur that came from the mouths of the horses were each able to kill.

9:19 The mouths of the horses kill; their tails wound.

9:20–21 The intent of the plagues is revealed. It is not vengeance—it is to lead humankind to repentance. And yet, despite the horror of the plagues, people still refuse to turn from their worship of demons and the lifestyle that such a commitment brings. *demons/idols.* They err in worshiping evil powers (demons) and/or dumb idols which have no life. In either case, this keeps them from worshiping the living God. Paul makes an interesting point when he asserts that demons stand behind dumb idols. To worship idols is to give oneself over to the demonic (1 Cor. 10:18–21).

UNIT 11—The Angel and the Little Scroll / Rev. 10:1–11

Scripture

The Angel and the Little Scroll

10 *Then I saw another mighty angel coming down from heaven. He was robed in a cloud, with a rainbow above his head; his face was like the sun, and his legs were like fiery pillars. ²He was holding a little scroll, which lay open in his hand. He planted his right foot on the sea and his left foot on the land, ³and he gave a loud shout like the roar of a lion. When he shouted, the voices of the seven thunders spoke. ⁴And when the seven thunders spoke, I was about to write; but I heard a voice from heaven say, "Seal up what the seven thunders have said and do not write it down."*

⁵Then the angel I had seen standing on the sea and on the land raised his right hand to heaven. ⁶And he swore by him who lives for ever and ever, who created the heavens and all that is in them, the earth and all that is in it, and the sea and all that is in it, and said, "There will be no more delay! ⁷But in the days when the seventh angel is about to sound his trumpet, the mystery of God will be accomplished, just as he announced to his servants the prophets."

⁸Then the voice that I had heard from heaven spoke to me once more: "Go, take the scroll that lies open in the hand of the angel who is standing on the sea and on the land."

⁹So I went to the angel and asked him to give me the little scroll. He said to me, "Take it and eat it. It will turn your stomach sour, but in your mouth it will be as sweet as honey." ¹⁰I took the little scroll from the angel's hand and ate it. It tasted as sweet as honey in my mouth, but when I had eaten it, my stomach turned sour. ¹¹Then I was told, "You must prophesy again about many peoples, nations, languages and kings."

Group Questions

TO BEGIN / 15 Minutes (Choose 1 or 2)

❏ Who was one of your heroes when you were a child? Why?
❏ What TV or movie hero is most popular with children today?
❏ What author or speaker is, in your opinion, a "hero" today?

READ SCRIPTURE AND DISCUSS / 30 Minutes

❏ Describe the angel who announces the coming of the seventh trumpet. In what ways does this picture contrast with the traditional view of angels? Why would John be forbidden to record the words of the seven thunders (see 2 Cor. 12:4)?
❏ What purposes did the disasters of the first six trumpets serve? What do you anticipate the seventh trumpet will bring forth? What is the "mystery" of God (v. 7; see Note 10:6; see also Rom. 11:25–36; 16:25–27; Eph. 1:9–14)?
❏ What happens to the small scroll? What does the eating symbolize? How can a revelation from God be both sweet and bitter?
❏ What is an experience you once savored for a moment, but later turned sour? How has God's Word been both sweet and sour to you?
❏ When has God led you into a project that you would not have selected for yourself? What happened?
❏ Who is the prophecy directed toward (v. 11)? How open are you right now to receiving God's instruction for your own life?

TO CLOSE AND PRAY / 15–30 Minutes

❏ How are you feeling about your time with this group in the book of Revelation? How is God challenging you through this study?
❏ What have you most appreciated about the group?
❏ What would you like this group to remember in prayer for you this week?

Notes

10:1–11:14 John inserts an extended interlude between the sixth and seventh trumpets, just as he did between the sixth and seventh seal. This interlude, like the other, has two parts to it. In part one, he relates the account of the mighty angel and the little scroll (10:1–11). In part two, he tells about measuring the temple and the two witnesses (11:1–14).

10:1 The description of this angel is so similar to that of Christ in chapter one that some commentators have identified him as such. However, in verse 6 he shows himself to be a genuine angel by swearing by "him who lives for ever and ever." ***robed in a cloud.*** Angels were described as ascending and descending on clouds (Ps. 104:3; Dan. 7:13; Acts 1:9), but this one is clothed in a cloud. ***rainbow.*** This can be understood as a kind of crown or as the reflection of his brilliance ("his face was like the sun") through the clouds. ***down from heaven.*** In 4:1 John was caught up to heaven, but now, it seems, he is back on earth and the angel descends to him. This is yet another example of the fluid language used in apocalyptic literature. This book must not be read as if it were an ordered, linear account to be interpreted like straight narrative.

10:2 ***a little scroll.*** This is an unusual word, used nowhere else in Greek literature prior to this time. John probably coined it himself. Unlike the scroll of 5:1 which was a book, this scroll was more akin to a booklet. ***open.*** Unlike that other scroll, the contents of this one were not hidden.

10:3 ***the seven thunders.*** No information is given as to the nature of these thunders.

10:4 John understood what the seven thunders communicated but he is told not to record them. What these thunders convey is, of course, unknown. But in each of the three other instances in Revelation where there is thunder, it is the precursor to judgment (8:5; 11:19; 16:18).

10:5 With the scroll in his left hand, the angel proceeds to lift his right hand toward heaven as he prepares to take an oath (see Deut. 32:40; Dan. 12:7).

10:6 What he swears is that there will be no more delay before the coming of the end. "From this point forward God will not intervene to give man further opportunity to repent. Restraint is to be removed and the Antichrist is to be revealed" (Mounce).

10:7 ***in the days when.*** The sounding of the seventh trumpet is not a single act but a period of time. As will emerge, it includes the events of the seven bowls (16:1–20). ***mystery of God.*** Mystery in the NT does not refer to something that is secret, but to the purpose of God which has been revealed.

10:8 ***the voice.*** The same voice that forbade John to record the words of the seven thunders (10:4) now tells him to take the scroll. ***the angel who is standing on the sea and on the land.*** For the third time the tremendous size of this angel is emphasized. His coming has something to do with all of the earth (see 10:2,5).

10:9 ***"Take it and eat it."*** Ezekiel was commanded to do the very same thing (Ezek. 2:9–3:3). Ezekiel is told to ingest the word of God, i.e. to assimilate it into his very being. This was a symbol of his commission to receive the word of God and then proclaim it. In the same way, John is (re-)commissioned to speak God's prophetic word in this end time (1:19).

10:10 ***sweet/sour.*** This message is both sweet (it is the word of God himself) and it is sour (it is a word of judgment against the people—see Psalm 19:8–10; 119:103; Ezekiel 3:3; Luke 19:41). To be called to be a prophet is not an unmixed blessing.

10:11 ***prophesy again.*** John has already given the prophecy of the seven seals and the six trumpets. He is to continue to prophesy as the end approaches. ***about many people.*** His message concerns the whole civilized world, not just the church or Israel or any other single nation.

UNIT 12—The Two Witnesses/The Seventh Trumpet / Revelation 11:1–19

Scripture

The Two Witnesses

11 *I was given a reed like a measuring rod and was told, "Go and measure the temple of God and the altar, and count the worshipers there. ²But exclude the outer court; do not measure it, because it has been given to the Gentiles. They will trample on the holy city for 42 months. ³And I will give power to my two witnesses, and they will prophesy for 1,260 days, clothed in sackcloth." ⁴These are the two olive trees and the two lampstands that stand before the Lord of the earth. ⁵If anyone tries to harm them, fire comes from their mouths and devours their enemies. This is how anyone who wants to harm them must die. ⁶These men have power to shut up the sky so that it will not rain during the time they are prophesying; and they have power to turn the waters into blood and to strike the earth with every kind of plague as often as they want.*

⁷Now when they have finished their testimony, the beast that comes up from the Abyss will attack them, and overpower and kill them. ⁸Their bodies will lie in the street of the great city, which is figuratively called Sodom and Egypt, where also their Lord was crucified. ⁹For three and a half days men from every people, tribe, language and nation will gaze on their bodies and refuse them burial. ¹⁰The inhabitants of the earth will gloat over them and will celebrate by sending each other gifts, because these two prophets had tormented those who live on the earth.

¹¹But after the three and a half days a breath of life from God entered them, and they stood on their feet, and terror struck those who saw them. ¹²Then they heard a loud voice from heaven saying to them, "Come up here." And they went up to heaven in a cloud, while their enemies looked on.

[Scripture continued on page 42]

Group Questions

TO BEGIN / 15 Minutes (Choose 1 or 2)

❏ What fire that you have seen or heard of has frightened you the most?

❏ Where would you least like to live: an area prone to earthquakes, hurricanes or floods?

❏ What is the greatest presentation of *Handel's Messiah* you have seen or heard?

READ SCRIPTURE AND DISCUSS / 30 Minutes

❏ What is John commanded to do in this passage? Why? According to the perspective assumed in these Notes, who will be "measured" (or protected), and why? With the church and the world set in contrast, what do the two indestructible witnesses represent? And their enemies?

❏ What happens to these two witnesses? Why? What results from their death and resurrection?

❏ What do you learn in this passage about what it means to be a witness? What has been toughest about living out your faith at work, school or home? Why is there such difficulty?

❏ In verse 15, what does this trumpet herald? How is the Second Coming a "good news/bad news" event?

❏ For what is God worshiped? What does this tell you about God's power?

❏ How do you react to God's power over unbelieving people: to *hurt* them (trumpet 5 or first woe—Rev. 9:1–11); to *kill* them (trumpet 6 or second woe—Rev. 9:12–22), or to *damn* them (trumpet 7 or third woe—Rev. 11:15–19)? Why?

❏ As God displays this power in response to prayers (8:4), how do you respond to what he has called you to do? What will you pray? Why?

TO CLOSE AND PRAY / 15–30 Minutes

❏ What have you sensed as God's job description for you in recent weeks or months? How do you feel about what he has called you to do? How have you been doing with this in the last week?

❏ Where do you need God's power in your life?

❏ How can this group pray for you?

Notes

11:1–14 This is the second part of the interlude: the story of measuring the temple and the two witnesses. This is an exceedingly difficult section to interpret. Four main lines of interpretation have been developed. First, many consider this to be an earlier piece of prophecy, written before 70 A.D., which tells of the literal, historical destruction of the temple by the Romans. However, it seems unlikely that John would have included a piece of apocalyptic writing from an earlier time, especially since some details had not been fulfilled (e.g., the inner courtyard [vv. 1–2] was not preserved from destruction by the Romans). Second, others think that this is a prophecy that is to be interpreted literally; namely, that at the end of the age the temple will be restored and will be the site of the struggle between restored Jews and the beast. The problem with this view is that elements of this passage are clearly symbolic (e.g. the measuring in verses 1–2 and the "great city" which verse 8 indicates is to be understood "figuratively"), and it is impossible to assert that certain features are literal (e.g., the restoration of the temple) while others are not. Third, some feel that this is a prediction of "the preservation of the Jewish people and their final salvation" (Ladd). Fourth, still others feel that this is a prophecy "about the fate of the witnessing church during its final period of opposition and persecution," akin to the sealing of the church in 7:1–8 (Mounce). This section cannot be analyzed (unfortunately) without adopting an interpretive perspective, and so the fourth alternative is assumed (with some tentativeness) in these notes.

11:1–2 l. John, who has been a passive spectator up to 10:8 (when he is given the scroll to eat), is asked to continue to be an active participant in the vision. *measure.* To measure is not simply to note the dimensions of the area. It is to set aside a place, either for destruction or for preservation (2 Kings 21:13; Isa. 34:11; Ezek. 40–43; Zech. 2:1–5). In this case, the area which John measures is to be preserved. *temple.* The Greek word refers to the temple building itself and not the outer courtyard. The temple itself consisted of a building at the center called the Holy of Holies, bordered by the court of the priests, the court of Israel, and the court of the women. These are where the people of Israel assembled. This temple complex was surrounded by a huge outer court where Gentiles were allowed to

come. What John is asked to measure is the inner, Jewish area. If the temple stands for the church (e.g., 1 Cor. 3:16–17; 2 Cor. 6:16; Eph. 2:19–22), then this is saying that it will be preserved during the coming destruction. *exclude the outer courtyard.* What this refers to is unclear. Possibly it means that although the church will be harmed physically (the outer court is trampled by the Gentiles), the church will not be harmed spiritually (the inner court). Christians may die, but they will not be severed from the life of God their Father. *trample on the holy city.* The holy city is another way of talking about the church. The church will be attacked but not destroyed. *42 months.* Three and a half years, the length of time evil is allowed to dominate (see Dan. 7:25; Rev. 11:2,3; 12:6,14; 13:5). The original reference in Daniel is probably to the period of time that the Jews suffered under the Syrian king Antiochus Epiphanes in 167–164 B.C. "Here is a fundamental clue to the understanding of biblical prophecy: eschatological events are foreshadowed in historical events" (Ladd).

11:3 *two witnesses.* What is clear is that these two men are modeled after Moses and Elijah (see 2 Kings 1:10–12; 1 Kings 17:1; Ex. 7:14–18; Mal. 4:5; Mark 9:4). In this context, they may be two individuals who preach repentance to Israel; or, more likely, they may be symbols of the witnessing church. During the time of domination of evil, witness to God continues. *sackcloth.* A coarse, dark cloth which signified mourning; it was the clothing often worn by prophets (Isa. 20:2; Zech. 13:4). *1,260 days.* Three and a half years = 42 months = 1,260 days (a solar month had 30 days).

11:4 The power for witness comes from the Spirit of God. See Zechariah 4 for the background to these symbols.

11:5–6 During the time of their prophetic activity, they are given supernatural powers which both protect them and enable them to judge the earth by their acts of power.

11:7 Once their ministry is completed, they are vulnerable to the beast of the Abyss. The scene portrayed here "is the last epic struggle between the kingdoms of this earth and the witnessing church"

[Notes continued on page 43]

[13]*At that very hour there was a severe earthquake and a tenth of the city collapsed. Seven thousand people were killed in the earthquake, and the survivors were terrified and gave glory to the God of heaven.*

[14]*The second woe has passed; the third woe is coming soon.*

The Seventh Trumpet

[15]*The seventh angel sounded his trumpet, and there were loud voices in heaven, which said:*

> *"The kingdom of the world has*
> *become the kingdom of our Lord*
> *and of his Christ,*
> *and he will reign for ever and ever."*

[16]*And the twenty-four elders, who were seated on their thrones before God, fell on their faces and worshiped God,* [17]*saying:*

> *"We give thanks to you, Lord God*
> *Almighty,*
> *the One who is and who was,*
> *because you have taken your great power*
> *and have begun to reign.*
> [18]*The nations were angry;*
> *and your wrath has come.*
> *The time has come for judging the dead,*
> *and for rewarding your servants the*
> *prophets*
> *and your saints and those who reverence*
> *your name,*
> *both small and great—*
> *and for destroying those who destroy the*
> *earth."*

[19]*Then God's temple in heaven was opened, and within his temple was seen the ark of his covenant. And there came flashes of lightning, rumblings, peals of thunder, an earthquake and a great hailstorm.*

(Mounce). **the beast.** This is the first time that this figure appears. He will become the major threat to the church in the last days (chapters 13; 17). His origins are clear: he is a demon out of the Abyss.

11:8 To be deprived of burial was considered a terrible thing. **the great city.** Morris maintains that this is symbolic and it "is every city and no city. It is civilized man in organized community." Thus it contains elements of Rome (which had become in that day the center of the world's power), and elements of Jerusalem (where the Lord was crucified), as well as "Sodom and Egypt" (which were symbols of wickedness, evil, and oppression—e.g., Gen. 19:1–11).

11:10–12 A holiday is declared now that those who tormented their consciences are dead. But the resurrection of the witnesses cuts short the rejoicing (see Ezek. 37). This is followed by the open, visible ascension into heaven of the witnesses (see 2 Kings 2:11).

11:13 This is followed by a devastating earthquake which levels a tenth of the city (see Ezek. 38:19–20). **gave glory to the God of heaven.** As other texts indicate this is probably not true repentance (e.g., 13:3–4) but rather an astonished acknowledgment of the power of God in response to the amazing resurrection of the witnesses. Still, as Caird says: "There seems … to be a good case for holding that John had wider hopes for the conversion of the world than he is commonly given credit for … Where retributive punishment had failed to bring men to repentance, the death of the martyrs would succeed."

11:15–19 Now that the background has been laid, the seventh and final trumpet can be sounded. However, before the impact of that trumpet is described, the final outcome of this event is declared: the kingdom of God has triumphed; it has been established (v. 15). In response, the elders sing an anthem of praise (vv. 16–18).

11:15 The rule of the world is now firmly and fully in the hands of God the Father and God the Son. This anticipates what will happen following the events described in the next chapters. **he will reign for ever and ever**. No more will Satan or evil disturb reality. Once his kingdom is established in fullness, God will reign from then on, uninterrupted.

11:17–18 The elders, in their praise, assert the same thing that has been proclaimed in 11:15—the redemptive work of God has been completed. They too look to the future when God's kingdom is established for all to see. **the nations were angry.** Before God's kingdom could come, power had to be taken away from those who were hostile to God (Ps. 2). **your wrath has come.** So God came in judgment (see Rev. 14:10–11; 16:15–21; 20:8–9). **judging the dead and rewarding your servants ... and saints.** "The judgment anticipated by the elders is carried out in the great white throne scene of 20:11–15. It is preceded by resurrection and followed by retribution. If the wrath of God is the judgment of the wicked, the vision of a New Jerusalem (21:9–22:5) with the presence of God its crowning joy (22:4) is the reward of the faithful" (Mounce). **saints.** Those who are God's people from all ages. **destroying those who destroy the earth.** It will also be a time when judgment is directed against those who have worked against God.

11:19 God's temple in heaven was opened. At the time of Jesus' death, the curtain in the temple in Jerusalem was torn in two, signifying that now men and women had free access to God (Matt. 27:51). That access, which was until this time spiritual, is now given concrete form. This opening up of the temple (along with the other events in vv. 15b–19) will, in fact, occur in chapters 21–22. But here, in this vision which speaks of the future as if it were the present, the outcome of end times is declared. **the ark of his covenant.** In the OT the ark of the covenant was a wooden chest which stood in the Holy of Holies and symbolized the presence of God. The ark was lost during one of the conflicts in Israel, but here it is restored as an indication of the fulfillment of the covenants God made with his people. **lightning, rumblings ... great hailstorm.** These signify the presence of God (see Note on 4:5).

UNIT 13—The Woman and the Dragon / Rev. 12:1–13:1a

Scripture

The Woman and the Dragon

12 *A great and wondrous sign appeared in heaven: a woman clothed with the sun, with the moon under her feet and a crown of twelve stars on her head. ²She was pregnant and cried out in pain as she was about to give birth. ³Then another sign appeared in heaven: an enormous red dragon with seven heads and ten horns and seven crowns on his heads. ⁴His tail swept a third of the stars out of the sky and flung them to the earth. The dragon stood in front of the woman who was about to give birth, so that he might devour her child the moment it was born. ⁵She gave birth to a son, a male child, who will rule all the nations with an iron scepter. And her child was snatched up to God and to his throne. ⁶The woman fled into the desert to a place prepared for her by God, where she might be taken care of for 1,260 days.*

⁷And there was war in heaven. Michael and his angels fought against the dragon, and the dragon and his angels fought back. ⁸But he was not strong enough, and they lost their place in heaven. ⁹The great dragon was hurled down—that ancient serpent called the devil, or Satan, who leads the whole world astray. He was hurled to the earth, and his angels with him.

¹⁰Then I heard a loud voice in heaven say:

"Now have come the salvation and the
power and the
kingdom of our God,
and the authority of his Christ.
For the accuser of our brothers,
who accuses them before our God day
and night,
has been hurled down.
¹¹They overcame him
by the blood of the Lamb
and by the word of their testimony;
they did not love their lives so much
as to shrink from death.

[Scripture continued on page 46]

Group Questions

TO BEGIN / 15 Minutes (Choose 1 or 2)

❑ Were you born before or after your mother's due date, or on time?
❑ When you were a child, who was the most important woman in your life other than your mother? Why?
❑ Who is the most important woman in your life today?

READ SCRIPTURE AND DISCUSS / 30 Minutes

❑ Describe the woman, the dragon and the child. Who does the woman represent? The dragon? The child?
❑ Where does the next conflict occur? Who are the protagonists? What is the outcome of this conflict? What is the significance of this outcome for the earth? For Christians? Which Old Testament and New Testament events are parallels to this passage?
❑ When do you see this heavenly battle occurring: At some particular time and place in history? Pre-history? Post-history? Any time and any place during the ongoing heavenly battle between the kingdoms of God and Satan (that is, in the spiritual realm which is behind all of this world's history)? Why do you think so?
❑ What do you learn here about conflict between the Christian church and demonic evil?
❑ When has Satan seemed very real to you? Why? How do you overcome Satan (see v. 11)? How could you apply these tactics in your own life? What do you need to do to become stronger for spiritual battle?

TO CLOSE AND PRAY / 15–30 Minutes

❑ What spiritual battle have you faced recently? Did you realize the battle was spiritual at the time?
❑ How can this group, and other friends, pray for you in the battles you are facing right now? Likewise, how can you pray for them?
❑ What battles are you facing that need powerful prayer? Share your prayer needs with the group.

TIME
FOR A
CHECK-UP

SEVEN COMMON SMALL GROUP AILMENTS
AND HOW TO OVERCOME THEM

ARE YOU FEELING A LITTLE

NERVOUS ABOUT BEING IN A SMALL GROUP?

SYMPTOMS: Do you break out into a sweat at the mention of small groups. Does your mouth turn to sawdust when it comes "your turn" to share? To pray?

PRESCRIPTION: Take this test to see if you are ready to belong to a small group. If you answer "yes" on seven out of ten questions below, you are probably ready to take the plunge.

1. Are you looking for a place where you can deal with the serious questions in your life right now?　☐ Yes　☐ No

2. Are you open to the possibility that God has something special for your life?
　☐ Yes　☐ No

3. Are you open to the Bible as the source where God's will for your life can be explored?
　☐ Yes　☐ No

4. Are you able to admit that you do not have all the answers about the Bible? God? Your own life?　☐ Yes　☐ No

5. Are you able to let others have questions about the Bible or God?　☐ Yes　☐ No

6. Are you willing to accept people in the group that are "Prodigal Sons" and have a long way to go in their spiritual faith?　☐ Yes　☐ No

7. Are you willing to keep anything that is shared in this group in strict confidence?　☐ Yes　☐ No

8. Are you willing to share in the responsibility for the group and to support group members with your prayers?　☐ Yes　☐ No

9. Are you willing to give priority to this group for a short period of time (such as six to twelve weeks) and consider making a longer commitment after this time?
　☐ Yes　☐ No

10. Are you excited about the possibilities of belonging to a group that could make a difference in your life?　☐ Yes　☐ No

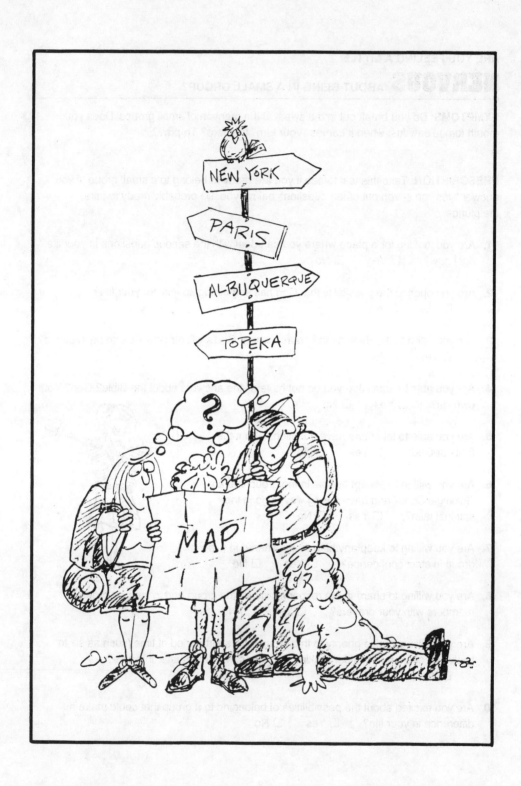

ARE YOU FEELING A LITTLE

CONFUSED ABOUT YOUR PURPOSE?

SYMPTOMS: Do you feel like you are playing on a team that doesn't have any rules? Any direction? Any idea of what you want to do or accomplish? Or where you are going?

PRESCRIPTION: Before you ever started the group, you should have decided on a COVENANT that spelled out your purpose, rules, expectations, etc. If you didn't, call "time out" and decide *together* on a covenant.

Here's how. Take the first sentence below and ask everyone to finish the sentence. Then, try to come up with a one sentence statement that you all can agree to. "The purpose of our group is . . ."

Then, take the second sentence and decide on your specific goals, etc. . . . until you have decided on your GROUP COVENANT. This becomes your game plan.

1. The purpose of our group is . . .

2. Our specific goals are . . .

3. We will meet _____ times, every _____ week, after which we will evaluate our group.

4. We will meet: Day of week _____ from _____ (time) to _____ .

5. We will meet at _____ , or rotate the place where we meet.

6. In addition to the study of the Bible, we will . . .

7. We will adhere to the following ground rules:
   - The leader of the group will be . . . or we will rotate the leadership.
   - The host for each meeting (other than the leader) will be . . . or we will rotate this responsibility.
   - Food/refreshments will be . . .
   - Baby-sitting, etc.

8. In addition to these general rules, we will agree to the following disciplines:
   - Attendance: To give priority to the group meetings
   - Participation: To share responsibility for the group
   - Confidentiality: To keep anything that is said strictly confidential
   - Accountability: To give permission to group members to hold you accountable for goals you set for yourself
   - Accessibility: To give one another the right to call upon you for help in time of need—even in the middle of the night.

ARE YOU FEELING A LITTLE

DISTANT FROM THE OTHERS IN YOUR GROUP?

SYMPTOMS: Does your group start off like a Model A Ford on a cold morning? Or sag in the middle when you get to the Bible study? Do you find some of the people do all the talking . . . and others never get out of their "shell"?

PRESCRIPTION: Use the "flow questions" in the margin, next to the Scripture text, to guide the discussion. The questions are carefully designed to explode like time bombs on three levels of sharing: (1) TO BEGIN—to break the ice, (2) READ SCRIPTURE AND DISCUSS—to discuss the Scripture text, and (3) TO CLOSE AND PRAY—to take inventory of your own life.

1 TO BEGIN / 10–15 Minutes: Start off with a few good "stories" about your childhood or human-interest experiences. The better the "stories" at this level . . . the deeper the group will share at the close. (There is a close parallel between "childlikeness" and "Christlikeness".)

TO BEGIN / 15 Minutes (Choose 1 or 2)
- ❏ What mail will you open first: Bills? Official looking stuff? Personal mail? Love letter?
- ❏ When you care for someone, are you more likely to send a funny card or a touching one?

2 READ SCRIPTURE AND DISCUSS / 30–45 Minutes: You read the Scripture text at this point and go around on the first question. The questions are designed both to get you into the text and to help you reflect on the Scripture's meaning for your own life. The questions will help to draw your group together in a way that all can participate and share. By the way, you do not have to finish all the questions. Save time for the TO CLOSE AND PRAY section.

READ SCRIPTURE AND DISCUSS / 30 Minutes
- ❏ Where is Paul writing from? Why? Who is he writing to? (Hint: Go back and read the Introduction, especially the paragraph on Origin and Occasion.)
- ❏ Who was the Apostle Paul in your spiritual life—who introduced you to Jesus Christ and cared about your spiritual growth?

3 TO CLOSE AND PRAY / 15–30 Minutes This is the heart of the Bible study. The purpose is to take inventory of your own life and share with the group "what God is telling you to do." The questions are "high risk"; that is, the group is asked to share on a "need level," before moving on to prayer.

TO CLOSE AND PRAY / 15-30 Minutes
- ❏ If you had a spiritual check-up today, what would the doctor prescribe?
- ❏ How can this Bible study group help you reach your spiritual goals?
- ❏ Who is someone you would like to invite to this group next week?
- ❏ What would you like this group to remember in prayer for you this week?

Scripture

Thanksgiving and Prayer

³I thank my God every time I remember you. ⁴In all my prayers for all of you, I always pray with joy ⁵because of your partnership in the gospel from the first day until now, ⁶being confident of this, that he who began a good work in you will carry it on to completion until the day of Christ Jesus. ⁷It is right for me to feel this way about all of you, since I have you in my heart;

Group Questions

TO BEGIN: What mail will you open first: Bills? Official looking stuff? Personal mail? Love letter?

READ SCRIPTURE AND DISCUSS: Where is Paul writing from? Why? Who is he writing to? (Hint: Go back and read the Introduction, especially the paragraph on Origin and Occasion).

TO CLOSE AND PRAY: If you had a spiritual check-up today, what would the doctor prescribe?

ARE YOU FEELING A LITTLE
INTIMIDATED BY THE BIBLE SCHOLARS IN YOUR GROUP?

SYMPTOMS: Are you afraid that your ignorance about the Bible could be embarrassing? For instance: if someone asked you who Melchizedek was, what would you say? If you said "an old linebacker for the Raiders", you would be wrong. Twice wrong.

PRESCRIPTION: Don't despair. Most of the people in your group don't know either. And that's O.K. This Bible study group is for BEGINNERS. And for BEGINNERS, there are Notes on the opposite page to help you keep up to speed with the rest of the group.

NOTES include:

- ☐ Definitions of significant words.

- ☐ Historical background: the political, social, economic context behind the words in the text.

- ☐ Geographical setting: facts about the country, terrain, lakes, crops, roads, and religious shrines.

- ☐ Cultural perspective: lifestyles, homes, customs, holidays, traditions, and social patterns.

- ☐ Archeological evidence: recent findings that sheds light on the Bible events.

- ☐ Summary/Commentary: recap of the argument to keep the passage in the context of the whole book.

Notes

1:3 *every time I remember you*. This is a difficult phrase to translate from the Greek. What it seems to mean is that during his times of prayer, Paul "was compelled by love to mention his Philippian friends. This means, then, that Paul gave thanks not whenever he happened to remember them, but that he regularly gave thanks for them and mentioned them to God at set times of prayer" (Hawthorne).

1:4 *with joy*. "Joy" is a theme that pervades Philippians. This is the first of some fourteen times that Paul will use the word in this epistle. He mentions "joy" more often in this short epistle

***confirming the gospel*.** These are legal terms. The reference is to Paul's defense before the Roman court, in which he hopes to be able not only to vindicate himself and the gospel from false charges, but to proclaim the gospel in life-changing power to those in the courtroom. (See Ac 26 for an example of how Paul did this when he stood in court before Agrippa and Festus.)

1:8 *I long*. Yet another word characteristic of Paul. He uses it seven of the nine times it is found in the New Testament. This is a strong word and expresses the depth of Paul's feelings for them, his desire to be with them, and the wish to minister

ARE YOU FEELING A LITTLE

TEMPTED TO KEEP THE GROUP JUST FOR YOURSELF?

SYMPTOMS: Two feelings surface: (1) if we let anyone into our group, it would destroy our "closeness", and/or (2) if we let anyone into our group, we would not have time enough to share.

PRESCRIPTION: Study the ministry of Jesus and the early church: the need for "closeness" and the danger of "closedness." How did Jesus respond to his own disciples when they asked to "stay together" and build a "monument." Note the Story of the Transfiguration in Mark 9:2–13.

SOLUTION #1: Pull up an empty chair during the prayer time at the close of the group and pray that God will "fill the chair" with someone by the next week.

SOLUTION #2: When the group reaches seven or eight in number, divide into two groups of 4—4 at the dining table, 4 at the kitchen table—when the time comes for the Bible study . . . and reshuffle the foursomes every week so that you keep the whole group intact, but sub-group for the discussion time.

THREE PART AGENDA FOR GROUP USING THE SUB-GROUP MODEL

GATHERING/15 Minutes/All Together.
Refreshments are served as the group
gathers and assignments are made to
sub-groups of 4.

SHARING/30–45 Minutes/Groups of 4.
Sub-groups are formed to discuss the
questions in the margin of the text.

CARING/15–30 Minutes/All Together.
Regather the whole group to share prayer
requests and pray.

ARE YOU FEELING A LITTLE

BORED WITH YOUR BIBLE STUDY GROUP?

SYMPTOMS: You feel "tired" before the meeting starts. And worse after it is over. The sharing is mostly a "head-trip". One person is absent three weeks in a row. Another is chronically late. You feel like your time could be better spent doing something else, but you don't know how to say it.

PRESCRIPTION: You may be having a group "mid-life" crisis. Here are three suggestions.

1. Call "time out" for a session and evaluate your Covenant (page 5). Are you focused on your "purpose"? Your goals? Are you sticking to your rules? Should you throw out some of your rules? (Nobody said you can't.)

2. Check to see if your group is hitting on all three cylinders for a healthy small group. (1) Nurture/Bible Study, (2) Support for one another, and (3) Mission/Task. Here's a way to test yourself.

   On a scale from 1 to 10, circle a number to indicate how you feel your group is doing on each of these three cylinders.

   ON NURTURE/BIBLE STUDY: Getting to know the Bible. Letting God speak to you about His plans for your life through the Scripture.

We're doing a LOUSY JOB	1	2	3	4	5	6	7	8	9	10	We're doing a GREAT JOB

   ON SUPPORT: Getting to know each other. Caring about each other. Holding each other accountable for the best God has for you.

We're doing a LOUSY JOB	1	2	3	4	5	6	7	8	9	10	We're doing a GREAT JOB

   ON MISSION/TASK: Reaching out to others in need. Drawing people into the group, or sponsoring another group.

We're doing a LOUSY JOB	1	2	3	4	5	6	7	8	9	10	We're doing a GREAT JOB

3. Consider the possibility that God is saying it is time to shut down the group. Take time for a party. Give everyone a chance to share what the group has meant to him/her and what he/she will remember most about the group.

ARE YOU FEELING A LITTLE

ITCHY ABOUT DOING SOMETHING MORE?

SYMPTOMS: You're feeling tired of just sitting around studying the Bible. You have friends who are really hurting. Struggling. God seems to be saying something, but you don't know just what.

PRESCRIPTION: Consider the possibility that God is asking your group to split up and give birth to some new groups. Here are some steps:

1. Brainstorm together. Go around and have everyone finish the first sentence below. Then, go around on the second sentence, etc.

   I am concerned about a group for . . . (such as . . . "a group for young mothers, single parents, blended families, parents of adolescents, men at my office, young couples, empty nesters . . ." etc.).

   I wish we could . . .

   I would be willing to . . .

2. Make a list of prospects (people from the fringe of the church or outside of any church) that you would like to invite to a dinner party at which you could explain "what this Bible study group has meant to you."

3. Write each of these people a hand-written invitation on your personal stationary, inviting them to the dinner party at your home. (Don't bother to use the church bulletin. Nobody reads that.)

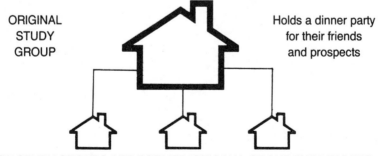

HOW TO TURN YOUR GROUP INTO A MISSIONARY GROUP

ORIGINAL
STUDY
GROUP

Holds a dinner party
for their friends
and prospects

NEW STUDY GROUPS ARE FORMED/ORIGINAL GROUP THE LEADERS

(P.S. You can still get back together with the whole group once a month for a "reunion" to share exciting "stories" of your new groups.

Notes

12:1–14:20 For the third time John inserts an interlude into his account. Between the account of the seven trumpets and the account of the seven bowls, he tells the story of the dragon and the woman (12:1–13:1a), the vision of the two great beasts (13:1b–18), and the vision of the Lamb on Mount Zion (14:1–20).

12:1–13:1a John describes, using a variety of symbols, the war in heaven between the forces of God and the forces of Satan. This explains why it is that the people of God have faced suffering and persecution down through the ages (John 16:33; Acts 14:22). It explains the intensification of the battle between good and evil during the Great Tribulation (Matt. 24:21). It also assures believers that the outcome of the battle is not in question. God has already won and that fact will soon be displayed for all to see. "This is not a vision of an event which is to take place at the end ... It is not meant to be a foretelling of history but a representation of the struggle in the spiritual world which lies behind history" (Ladd). Interestingly, certain parallels to this account can be found in the folklore of other cultures. Various peoples were aware, it seems, that a cosmic battle of this sort lay behind history.

12:1 *a sign.* John looks up and sees in the sky a portent. *a woman.* The first participant in this heavenly drama is introduced: the radiant woman who represents the idealized Israel, the mother of the people of the God (Isa. 54:1; 66:7–8; Gal. 4:26). "The woman is the ideal church in heaven; her children are the actual historical people of God on earth" (Ladd). The details of her dress indicate her magnificence. Psalm 104:2 describes God in such terms. *a crown of twelve stars.* Perhaps this symbolizes the 12 tribes (Gen. 37:9).

12:2 She is the mother of the Messiah (v. 5; see Isa. 26:17; 66:7–8; Mic. 4:10; 5:3) and also the church (v. 17).

12:3 *red dragon.* The second participant comes on stage: the great dragon who is Satan (v. 9). The dragon/serpent is seen as the embodiment of evil in the OT (see Ps. 74:14; Isa. 27:1; 51:9). *ten horns.* See Daniel 7:7. *seven crowns.* Seven is the number

of completeness; a crown is the sign of power. Satan is a figure of enormous power. *heads.* His seven heads indicate great intelligence as well.

12:4 *swept a third of the stars.* Another sign of his enormous power. *devour her child.* The purpose of Satan is revealed: He wants to destroy the Messiah.

12:5 *a male child.* The third participant appears. The language used to describe him clearly indicates that he is the Messiah (Ps. 2:9; Rev. 2:27; 19:15). *snatched up to God.* No specific events in the life of Christ are conveyed in the descriptions in this verse (this is not his actual birth nor Herod's attempt to destroy him nor his ascension, though all these events show the truth of this account). All this takes place in the heavens. The point of the verse is that he escapes the dragon.

12:6 Frustrated in its attempt to devour the child, the dragon turns on the mother but she is protected by God, as the church on earth will be during the three and one half years when the dragon is loose on earth. *desert.* This is not a wasteland but a place of refuge (as it often was for the children of Israel).

12:7–9 The focus shifts to the war in heaven, the point of which is to show that Satan is defeated. Again, no detail of history is intended. This does not describe the fall of Satan nor the conflict between the church and Satan in this world. "The single intent of the passage is to assure those who meet satanic evil on earth that it is really a defeated power, however contrary it might seem to human experience" (Ladd). *Michael.* See Daniel 12:1. *that ancient serpent.* An allusion to Genesis 3:1–5. *the devil.* Literally, *diabolos*, a Greek term for Satan meaning "accuser," "adversary," or "slanderer" (Zech. 3:1–2; 1 Peter 5:8). *Satan.* A Hebrew term meaning "adversary" (Job 1:6).

12:10 This announcement, like that in 11:15, states in the present what will be accomplished in the future.

12:11 The source of Satan's defeat is now announced: It came via the death of Jesus on the cross. That defeat continues to be manifested by the

[Notes continued on page 47]

[12]Therefore rejoice, you heavens
and you who dwell in them!
But woe to the earth and the sea,
because the devil has gone down to
you!
He is filled with fury,
because he knows that his time is
short."

[13]When the dragon saw that he had been hurled to the earth, he pursued the woman who had given birth to the male child. [14]The woman was given the two wings of a great eagle, so that she might fly to the place prepared for her in the desert, where she would be taken care of for a time, times and half a time, out of the serpent's reach. [15]Then from his mouth the serpent spewed water like a river, to overtake the woman and sweep her away with the torrent. [16]But the earth helped the woman by opening its mouth and swallowing the river that the dragon had spewed out of his mouth. [17]Then the dragon was enraged at the woman and went off to make war against the rest of her offspring—those who obey God's commandments and hold to the testimony of Jesus.

13 *And the dragon[a] stood on the shore of the sea.*

[a]1 Some late manuscripts *And I*

Notes (Continued)

word of testimony of those who were martyrs; i.e., those who followed in Christ's footsteps and were faithful unto death.

12:12 The defeat of Satan has two results. There is rejoicing in heaven among those who are of God, but there is woe on earth because Satan will now exercise his power there. *woe to earth.* Some say that this is the third woe announced in 8:13.

12:13–16 John now picks up again the story of the woman and the dragon. Satan follows the woman into the wilderness, where she has been safeguarded for three and a half years (v. 6). The events in this story are parallel to certain events in the story of the Exodus. "The pursuit of the woman is similar to Pharaoh's pursuit of the children of Israel as they fled from Egypt (Ex. 14:8). The two wings of the great eagle which made possible her escape echo the words of God from Sinai, 'I bore you on eagles' wings and brought you to myself' (Ex. 19:4). The river of water which flowed from the dragon's mouth may reflect Pharaoh's charge to drown the male children of the Israelites in the Nile (Ex. 1:22). The opening of the earth is reminiscent of the destruction of the men of Korah when in the wilderness they were swallowed by the earth and went down alive into Sheol (Num. 16:1–33)" (Mounce).

12:14 She escapes by means of a pair of eagle wings that she is given (see Deut. 32:10–11; Isa. 40:31). Once again, the assurance is given to the church that it will be preserved. *a time, times and half a time.* One year plus two years plus a half a year. This phrase is taken from Daniel 7:25, and is the same time period as three and a half years = 42 months = 1,260 days (see note for 11:2).

12:15–16 In the OT, a flood is sometimes used as a metaphor for an overwhelming trial (e.g., Ps. 18:4; Isa. 43:2).

12:17 The woman has already given birth to the Messiah and he has escaped Satan (v. 5). Now Satan turns his wrath on her other children (who, in this metaphor, are God's people). They already have victory over Satan (v.10), but Satan can still harm them. This is John's word of encouragement to the church in his time: Satan, indeed, may persecute you, but in reality he has already been defeated.

13:1a In order to carry out his war against the offspring of the woman, Satan stands on the shore of the sea to wait for the beast who will be his means of persecuting the church.

UNIT 14—The Beast out of the Sea / The Beast out of the Earth / Revelation 13:1b–18

Scripture

The Beast out of the Sea

And I saw a beast coming out of the sea. He had ten horns and seven heads, with ten crowns on his horns, and on each head a blasphemous name. ²The beast I saw resembled a leopard, but had feet like those of a bear and a mouth like that of a lion. The dragon gave the beast his power and his throne and great authority. ³One of the heads of the beast seemed to have had a fatal wound, but the fatal wound had been healed. The whole world was astonished and followed the beast. ⁴Men worshiped the dragon because he had given authority to the beast, and they also worshiped the beast and asked, "Who is like the beast? Who can make war against him?"

⁵The beast was given a mouth to utter proud words and blasphemies and to exercise his authority for forty-two months. ⁶He opened his mouth to blaspheme God, and to slander his name and his dwelling place and those who live in heaven. ⁷He was given power to make war against the saints and to conquer them. And he was given authority over every tribe, people, language and nation. ⁸All inhabitants of the earth will worship the beast—all whose names have not been written in the book of life belonging to the Lamb that was slain from the creation of the world.[a]

⁹He who has an ear, let him hear.

¹⁰If anyone is to go into captivity,
into captivity he will go.
If anyone is to be killed[b] *with the sword, with the sword he will be killed.*

This calls for patient endurance and faithfulness on the part of the saints.

[Scripture continued on page 50]

a8 Or *written from the creation of the world in the book of life belonging to the Lamb that was slain* b10 Some manuscripts *anyone kills*

Group Questions

TO BEGIN / 15 Minutes (Choose 1 or 2)

❏ When you were growing up, who was the most patient person in your family? What impressed you about his or her patience?
❏ Who is one of the most outgoing members of your family?
❏ Who do you think is one of the most charismatic leaders living today? How has charisma helped him or her to lead?

READ SCRIPTURE AND DISCUSS / 30 Minutes

❏ What is this beast from the sea like? What is the source of its power? How does it use its power? What is the extent of its power? What is the relationship between the beast and the dragon?
❏ Who worships the beast?
❏ Who would have been identified as this beast by the first-century Christians (see Dan. 7 and Rom. 13:1, see also Note 13:2)?
❏ What impact will this beast have on Christians? How ought they to respond? Why?
❏ In verses 11–17, what is the beast from the earth like?
❏ If the first beast exercises political power, what authority does this second beast exercise? How are true government and religion connected to (and mimicked by) these two beasts?
❏ Who are some of the beasts or idols in your life (people, forces, institutions, etc.) that test your allegiance to Christ? How have you been swayed from your allegiance to Christ by talk of "patriotism" and "tradition"? How is God helping you to deal with that?
❏ Since "7" is the number of completeness in Revelation, what might "666" mean?
❏ Compare the view of the Roman Empire here with the one in Romans 13:1–7. How had Rome changed since Paul's day? How can we discern false religion and governments?
❏ Is your name written in the Book of Life? How do you know?

TO CLOSE AND PRAY / 15–30 Minutes

❏ What has tried your patience during the last week? What grade would you give yourself on patient endurance and faithfulness? Why?
❏ Since beginning this study of Revelation, how has your view of the trials in your life changed? How has your view of God changed?
❏ What are your prayer needs this week?

Notes

13:1b–18 John recounts the works of the two beasts: the one from the sea (13:1b–10) and the one from the earth (13:11–18). "Together with the dragon the two beasts constitute an unholy trinity of malicious evil" (Mounce).

13:1b *a beast.* This is the Antichrist. The idea of the Antichrist is found throughout the Bible. The first mention is in Daniel 7, where he makes war against God's people. Jesus spoke of "the abomination that causes desolation" who will persecute God's people (Mark 13:14). Paul called this figure "the man of lawlessness" because he will oppose God (2 Thess. 2:3–4). He is inspired by Satan and he will seek to deceive people (2 Thess. 2:9–10). In his first epistle, John says that antichrists have already come, referring probably to the precursors of the final Antichrist (1 John 2:18–27). He urges the people to test the spirits lest they be taken in by the spirit of antichrist, which he defines as that which does not acknowledge that Jesus is from God (1 John 4:1–6). In Revelation 11:7, the beast comes out of the Abyss and thus shows himself to be demonic. "The beast represents both every hostile evil power that opposes and persecutes God's people, but primarily the eschatological figure at the end of the age" (Ladd). Though discussed in metaphorical terms, such embodiments of evil are understood by John to be very real and quite active in the world. They are a genuine danger to those who seek to follow God. *out of the sea.* The sea was often considered to be a place of evil. *seven heads, with ten crowns on his horns.* Like the dragon, the beast has multiple heads and horns. There is a difference, however. The dragon has seven crowns on his heads (see Note on 12:3), while the beast has 10 crowns on his horns. These 10 crowns represent 10 kings (17:12). *on each head a blasphemous name.* The beast has taken to himself divine names. In verse 4 he is worshiped. This accords with Paul's description of the man of lawlessness: "He will oppose and will exalt himself over everything that is called God or is worshiped, so that he sets himself up in God's temple, proclaiming himself to be God" (2 Thess. 2:4). "This self-deification of Antichrist has had its precursors in history. Deification of the emperor was prominent in the Roman Empire. Julius Caesar, Augustus,

Claudius, Vespasian, and Titus had been pronounced divine by the Roman Senate after their death ... The most explicit claim to deity was made by Domitian (A.D. 81–96) who demanded that he be addressed by the title, Dominus et Deus–Lord and God" (Ladd). Mounce adds to this: "There is little doubt that for John the beast was the Roman Empire as persecutor of the church. It was that spirit of imperial power which claimed a religious sanction for its gross injustices. Yet the beast is more than the Roman Empire. John's vision grew out of the details of his own historical situation, but its complete fulfillment awaits the final denouement of human history. The beast has always been and will be in a final intensified manifestation, the deification of secular authority."

13:2 This beast has all the attributes of the four beasts in Daniel 7. He is the embodiment of evil, in that his power is derived from Satan. In Daniel, these beasts represent four kingdoms which were hostile to God. "For John the Roman Empire was so satanic and terrible that in itself it included all the evil terrors of the evil empires which had gone before. It was, as it were, the sum total of all evil" (Barclay).

13:3 The beast was slain but later revived (see 13:14). This parallels the fate of the Lamb who was slain (5:6).

13:4 *they also worshiped the beast.* Arrayed against God and the Messiah are the dragon (Satan) and the beast (the Antichrist) in a kind of supernatural symmetry, continuing the parallelism begun in verse 3. They set themselves up as counterfeit deities. The aim of the beast is not just political power as the crowns suggest, but religious power. He seeks to gain the allegiance of the people and so subvert them from worship of the true God.

13:5 Thus the beast speaks as if he were God, in accord with Daniel 7:8,20,25. *given a mouth.* The beast is controlled by a higher power. *42 months.* Once again the same number appears. This is the length of time of the great persecution. See Note on 11:2.

[Notes continued on page 51]

Scripture (Continued)

The Beast out of the Earth

[11]Then I saw another beast, coming out of the earth. He had two horns like a lamb, but he spoke like a dragon. [12]He exercised all the authority of the first beast on his behalf, and made the earth and its inhabitants worship the first beast, whose fatal wound had been healed. [13]And he performed great and miraculous signs, even causing fire to come down from heaven to earth in full view of men. [14]Because of the signs he was given power to do on behalf of the first beast, he deceived the inhabitants of the earth. He ordered them to set up an image in honor of the beast who was wounded by the sword and yet lived. [15]He was given power to give breath to the image of the first beast, so that it could speak and cause all who refused to worship the image to be killed. [16]He also forced everyone, small and great, rich and poor, free and slave, to receive a mark on his right hand or on his forehead, [17]so that no one could buy or sell unless he had the mark, which is the name of the beast or the number of his name.

[18]This calls for wisdom. If anyone has insight, let him calculate the number of the beast, for it is man's number. His number is 666.

Notes (Continued)

13:6 blaspheme. By its words, he claims to possess that which belong to God alone. This is the essence of blasphemy: playing at being God.

13:7 The beast turns his wrath against the people of God. This is a time of great persecution. This verse does not mean that the beast succeeded in turning the saints from allegiance to God to allegiance to himself; only that he was able to kill them. However, as it turns out, these martyrs have, in fact, won a great victory (15:2). **he was given authority.** The beast was allowed for this period of time to control the world.

13:8 All are required to worship the beast. The exception are those who belong to the Lamb, who will die as martyrs as a result of their refusal to worship. **the book of life.** The registry of all who have been saved by faith in the crucified Lamb.

13:9 This was a phrase used often by Jesus when he wanted people to pay special attention so as to grasp the crucial thing he was teaching (see Matt. 11:15).

13:10 There are two ways this proverb can be read. Taking the alternative (see NIV footnote), Mounce comments: "The first couplet teaches that the believer must accept what God has ordained, and the second warns against any attempt on the part of the church to defend itself by the use of force." **patient endurance and faithfulness.** Retribution will come, but not immediately. They must wait for that day.

13:11–18 A second beast arises who is a servant to the first beast. His purpose is to cause people to worship the first beast. He is probably meant to represent organized religion. He is later called the false prophet (16:3; 19:20; 20:10). "The first beast represents civil power, satanically inspired; the second beast represents religious power employed to support civil power" (Ladd). In the first century, this would have been the imperial priesthood that served to promote emperor worship. With the coming of this beast, the evil trinity is complete. Satan, the Antichrist, and the false prophet oppose God the Father, Son, and the Holy Spirit.

13:11 two horns like a lamb. The second beast is a parody of Christ: a beast pretending to be a lamb. **spoke like a dragon.** His voice gave away his true identity (Matt. 7:15).

13:13–15 The second beast has power, but it is power derived from Satan (see 2 Thess. 2:9–10). This would be akin to magic. **was given power.** In the same way that in 13:5–7 (when speaking about the first beast) the passive "was given" is used four times (in the Greek text) emphasizing that the first beast was a front for Satan, so too here the point is made that this second beast has no independent power. It also is controlled by Satan. **an image in honor of the beast.** He had a statue made of the first beast and used his power to make it speak. There were stories in the ancient world about statues that could speak. The intention behind this pseudomiracle is to mimic the power of God to bring life. **cause ... to be killed.** It is the statute that commands the death of those who will not worship it, in this battle between God and Satan.

13:16 Satan continues to mimic God and his ways (see notes on 13:3 and 13:4). Here he causes people to be sealed with the name of the beast, just as God's people were sealed with God's mark in 7:3. Now there are people sealed for God and those sealed for Satan. **mark.** Brands were put on animals. Some slaves were similarly marked with the name of their owner; certain religious devotees were tattooed. This term also referred to the imperial seal that was used on official documents and on coins.

13:17 There are severe economic consequences for failing to have the mark of the beast. Such people cannot purchase anything, nor can they engage in trade.

13:18 666. Many attempts have been made to translate this number into a name. None really succeed, since all such translation is, in the end, guesswork. Some suggest that this is a symbol not a cryptogram, and that since 7 is the perfect number, each number in the mark falls short of such perfection. Satan and his kin try to mimic God but fall short.

UNIT 15—The Lamb and the 144,000/The Three Angels/ The Harvest of the Earth / Rev. 14:1–20

Scripture

The Lamb and the 144,000

14 Then I looked, and there before me was the Lamb, standing on Mount Zion, and with him 144,000 who had his name and his Father's name written on their foreheads. *²And I heard a sound from heaven like the roar of rushing waters and like a loud peal of thunder. The sound I heard was like that of harpists playing their harps. ³And they sang a new song before the throne and before the four living creatures and the elders. No one could learn the song except the 144,000 who had been redeemed from the earth. ⁴These are those who did not defile themselves with women, for they kept themselves pure. They follow the Lamb wherever he goes. They were purchased from among men and offered as firstfruits to God and the Lamb. ⁵No lie was found in their mouths; they are blameless.*

The Three Angels

⁶Then I saw another angel flying in midair, and he had the eternal gospel to proclaim to those who live on the earth—to every nation, tribe, language and people. ⁷He said in a loud voice, "Fear God and give him glory, because the hour of his judgment has come. Worship him who made the heavens, the earth, the sea and the springs of water."

⁸A second angel followed and said, "Fallen! Fallen is Babylon the Great, which made all the nations drink the maddening wine of her adulteries."

⁹A third angel followed them and said in a loud voice: "If anyone worships the beast and his image and receives his mark on the forehead or on the hand, ¹⁰he, too, will drink of the wine of God's fury, which has been poured full strength into the cup of his wrath. He will be tormented with burning sulfur in the presence of the holy angels and of the Lamb.

Group Questions

TO BEGIN / 15 Minutes (Choose 1 or 2)

❑ When have you been on a farm? What kind of farm was it?

❑ When have you seen sheep and lambs? Were they grazing or in captivity?

❑ What have you "harvested" in a garden?

READ SCRIPTURE AND DISCUSS / 30 Minutes

❑ Given the chaos described in chapters 12–13, what comfort do you find in this passage? What sight? Sounds? Feelings?

❑ Who is the Lamb? What has he done? Why are the people following him?

❑ How are you like (and unlike) the 144,000? Why do you follow the Lamb?

❑ In verses 6–7, what is the essence of the "eternal gospel" proclaimed by the angel of grace? Who will hear it? Has this vision yet been fulfilled? What response to the Gospel is called for?

❑ What have you done to help proclaim the Gospel to every nation, tribe, language and people (v. 6)?

❑ By contrast, what message does the angel of doom spread? Who is the fallen Babylon? Who has been infected by the spirit of Babylon?

❑ How does Satan's system (13:2–10) differ from God's church (14:1–5)? How does Satan's ideology (13:11–18) differ from God's truth (14:6–13)?

❑ How do you look upon death: As a rest? A reward? A new phase in the journey? What would you like to be doing when God calls you home?

❑ In verses 14–20, identify the four supernatural beings in this fifth vision. What is the role of each?

❑ What are the differences between the two parts of the vision (vv. 14–16 and 17–20)? What is the nature of the judgment that will occur (see Matt. 13:30,39)?

❑ Who does the figure "like the son of man" represent? (See Dan. 7:13). What does the harvesting of grapes usually represent in the Bible? (See Note 14:18).

❑ How is the portrayal of angels in this passage different from the way angels are portrayed in our society today?

❑ Regarding the harvest of the earth, how ripe do you think the world is now? Do you feel that the end of the world is close at hand? Why or why not? How does this affect your life?

[Scripture and Group Questions continued on page 54]

Notes

14:1–20 In the interlude between the seven trumpets and the seven bowls, John continues to fill in the background out of which the final judgment will emerge. In this final section before the bowls of wrath are poured out, John describes a series of visions, each of which serve to assure his readers that the wicked will be judged and that the saints will be saved.

14:1–5 The first of these visions concerns the Lamb on Mount Zion with the 144,000 who bear his mark. This stands in sharp contrast to the previous vision of the beast and those who bear his mark. Once again (see 10:7; 11:15), it is a vision of the future after the judgment (that is spoken of as if it were happening then and there) is over. This vision will come to pass in chapters 20–22. It also parallels the vision in 7:9–17.

14:1 *Mount Zion.* In the vision of Joel, this is the place of deliverance for those who call upon the name of the Lord (Joel 2:32). This is the heavenly Zion, the Jerusalem that is above (Gal. 4:26; Heb. 12:22) since this whole scene takes place in a heavenly context.

14:4 Many take this verse to mean that the 144,000 are a special class of people who enjoy a special relationship with God and who are characterized by three things: abstinence from marriage (celibacy); following of the Lamb; and special consecration to God. Others consider that "they are to be taken as the entire body of the redeemed" (Mounce). ***did not defile themselves with women.*** It is true that both Jesus and Paul spoke approvingly of those who abstained from marriage (Matt. 19:12; 1 Cor. 7:1,32) but they also spoke approvingly of marriage (Matt. 19:4–6; Eph. 5:31–32). Furthermore, Israel was spoken of as a virgin in the OT (2 Kings 19:21; Jer. 18:13; Lam. 2:13; Amos 5:2), as was the church in the NT (2 Cor. 11:2). Therefore this phrase can be taken in a figurative sense, in which case the 144,000 would be the church (the spotless bride of Christ), who have not defiled themselves with the hostile world systems. ***pure.*** This word can be translated "pure" or "chaste," and can refer to spiritual purity. John speaks of being aligned with the beast as "fornication" (14:8; 17:2; 18:3,9; 19:2). The concept of spiritual adultery is also found in the OT (e.g.,

Jer. 3:6; Hos. 2:5). So this probably means that these people were the ones who kept themselves pure by not worshiping the beast. ***they follow the Lamb.*** The 144,000 are not just characterized by what they did not do—they are also men and women who followed the teaching and instructions of Jesus. They lived out his lifestyle (Mark 8:34). ***firstfruits.*** Originally this was an offering to God of some of the fruit from the beginning of the harvest (Lev. 23:9–14). In the NT, the term is used figuratively of the first converts in an area (Rom. 16:5), and literally of Christ as the first one to rise from the dead (1 Cor. 15:20). Both Israel and the church were spoken of in this way (Jer. 2:3; James 1:18).

14:6–13 The next vision has to do with three angels. The first proclaims the Gospel (14:6–7); the second announces the Fall of Babylon (14:8); and the third reveals the fate of those who follow the beast (14:9–11).

14:6–7 The visions in chapter 14 are not in chronological order. 14:1–5 is about the final salvation of God's people, while here the angel calls men and women to belief in God. ***midair.*** So all could see and hear him. ***to those who live on earth.*** Again (e.g., 3:10; 6:10; 8:13) this refers to the people who do not worship and follow God. The angel is calling them to change their minds and ways and come to God. Yet again, on the eve of judgment, an appeal is made to those who stand outside God's kingdom. ***him who made the heavens.*** In the face of the powers of the beast, the angel asserts that it is God who made all of creation.

14:8 This is another announcement of what is yet to come (see 11:15; 12:10) as if it had just happened (17:1–18:24). ***Babylon.*** The original Babylon was a great city in Mesopotamia, renowned for its luxury and its corruption. It was also the traditional enemy of Israel. Here Babylon "stands for the capital city of the final apostate civilization, the symbol of human society organized politically, economically, and religiously in opposition to and defiance of God" (Ladd). In first-century terms, "Babylon" was Rome, the center of opposition to Christianity. ***wine of her adulteries.*** Rome seduced the nations by her power, luxury and corruption (17:2).

[Notes continued on page 55]

Scripture (Continued)

[11]And the smoke of their torment rises for ever and ever. There is no rest day or night for those who worship the beast and his image, or for anyone who receives the mark of his name." [12]This calls for patient endurance on the part of the saints who obey God's commandments and remain faithful to Jesus.

[13]Then I heard a voice from heaven say, "Write: Blessed are the dead who die in the Lord from now on."

"Yes," says the Spirit, "they will rest from their labor, for their deeds will follow them."

The Harvest of the Earth

[14]I looked, and there before me was a white cloud, and seated on the cloud was one "like a son of man"[a] with a crown of gold on his head and a sharp sickle in his hand. [15]Then another angel came out of the temple and called in a loud voice to him who was sitting on the cloud, "Take your sickle and reap, because the time to reap has come, for the harvest of the earth is ripe." [16]So he who was seated on the cloud swung his sickle over the earth, and the earth was harvested.

[17]Another angel came out of the temple in heaven, and he too had a sharp sickle. [18]Still another angel, who had charge of the fire, came from the altar and called in a loud voice to him who had the sharp sickle, "Take your sharp sickle and gather the clusters of grapes from the earth's vine, because its grapes are ripe." [19]The angel swung his sickle on the earth, gathered its grapes and threw them into the great winepress of God's wrath. [20]They were trampled in the winepress outside the city, and blood flowed out of the press, rising as high as the horses' bridles for a distance of 1,600 stadia.[b]

Group Questions (Continued)

TO CLOSE AND PRAY / 15–30 Minutes

❑ On a scale of 1 to 10, how closely have you been walking with Jesus this week? What has taken your attention away from him?

❑ What would you like to do this week in order to walk more closely with him?

❑ How can this group support you in prayer this week?

---

[a]14 Daniel 7:13   [b]20 That is, about 180 miles (about 300 kilometers)

Notes (Continued)

14:9–11 The third angel discloses the fate of those who do not leave the beast and worship God. In contrast to 13:15–17 (where those who do not worship the beast are killed and those without the mark of the beast are cut out of society), here those who worship the beast and bear his mark will be the objects of God's wrath. ***burning sulfur.*** The lake of fire and brimstone is the symbol used in Revelation for the final resting place of Satan and his cohorts and followers (20:10,14–15). ***in the presence of the holy angels and of the Lamb.*** See Mark 8:38; Luke 12:9. ***their torment rises for ever and ever.*** See Matthew 25:46. "After due allowance is made for the place of symbolism in apocalyptic, what remains in these verses is still the terrifying reality of divine wrath poured out upon those who persist in following Antichrist" (Mounce).

14:12 This is not part of the angel's cry, but rather a comment following it. It was not easy to live in the realm of the beast, but faced with implications of what it meant to be his follower in verses 9–11, the saint is encouraged to hang on and endure.

14:13 This idea is reinforced by the voice from heaven. Such endurance may well result in death, but the death of a saint is a death with a good outcome: eternal rest and reward for faithfulness. ***Blessed.*** This is the second of seven beatitudes found in Revelation (see 1:3; 16:15; 19:9; 20:6; 22:7,14). ***from now on.*** This is not to say that those who died before the Great Tribulation fail to be so blessed; it simply reminds those who are facing this terrible persecution that this is what awaits them. ***rest from their labor.*** This is not rest from ordinary work, but the cessation of the trials confronting those who seek to remain faithful to Jesus in the midst of a hostile kingdom.

14:14–20 The final two images in this chapter deal with harvest: the harvest of grain (14:14–16) and the harvest of grapes (14:17–20). Both are images of the final judgment (Jer. 51:33; Hos. 6:11; Mark 4:29; Matt. 13:39).

14:14 *one "like a son of man."* This title comes originally from Daniel 7:13–14; it was used extensively by Jesus as a title for himself (e.g., Mark 2:10). Here it identifies the Messiah who comes in judgment (Matt. 13:37–43; 25:31–46).

14:15 *out of the temple.* The command to begin the judgment comes from God himself in his holy temple. *the harvest.* The image of harvest in the NT carries the idea both of gathering people into God's kingdom (Matt. 9:37–38) and of gathering the wicked for divine judgment (Matt. 13:30,40–42). "The figure is comprehensive, including in a word the whole process of the winding up of the ages, and the recompense of both the good and the bad" (Beckwith).

14:16 This reaping will be described in chapters 19–20.

14:17–20 If the first image has to do with the gathering in of all people (both those who are the followers of God and those who are the followers of the beast), clearly the second image is about the judgment of the wicked.

14:18 The idea of harvesting grapes is used elsewhere in the Bible as an image for judgment (see Isa. 63:2–6; Joel 3:13).

14:19 Clearly judgment, not salvation, is in mind. The grapes are tossed into a huge winepress to be trampled upon. *winepress.* In those days, grapes were placed in a vat cut out of rock about eight feet square with a channel leading to another vat. Grapes were tossed into the upper vat and people walked about on them, squashing the grapes into juice.

14:20 The image shifts from wine to blood. The amount of blood is enormous. *as high as the horses' bridles.* About four feet deep. *1,600 stadia.* Some 184 miles (the approximate length of Palestine).

UNIT 16—Seven Angels With Seven Plagues / Rev. 15:1–8

Scripture

Seven Angels With Seven Plagues

15 *I saw in heaven another great and marvelous sign: seven angels with the seven last plagues—last, because with them God's wrath is completed. ²And I saw what looked like a sea of glass mixed with fire and, standing beside the sea, those who had been victorious over the beast and his image and over the number of his name. They held harps given them by God ³and sang the song of Moses the servant of God and the song of the Lamb:*

> *"Great and marvelous are your deeds,*
> *Lord God Almighty.*
> *Just and true are your ways,*
> *King of the ages.*
> *⁴Who will not fear you, O Lord,*
> *and bring glory to your name?*
> *For you alone are holy.*
> *All nations will come*
> *and worship before you,*
> *for your righteous acts have been*
> *revealed."*

⁵After this I looked and in heaven the temple, that is, the tabernacle of the Testimony, was opened. ⁶Out of the temple came the seven angels with the seven plagues. They were dressed in clean, shining linen and wore golden sashes around their chests. ⁷Then one of the four living creatures gave to the seven angels seven golden bowls filled with the wrath of God, who lives for ever and ever. ⁸And the temple was filled with smoke from the glory of God and from his power, and no one could enter the temple until the seven plagues of the seven angels were completed.

Group Questions

TO BEGIN / 15 Minutes (Choose 1 or 2)

❑ Growing up, what did your family's dishes look like?
❑ When did you take a vacation to a lake, river or the ocean?
❑ Which of these bodies of water is most calming to you? Why?

READ SCRIPTURE AND DISCUSS / 30 Minutes

❑ How does John describe this new sign? Why does he say these are the last plagues?
❑ What picture does he paint in verse 2? Compare Moses' song of deliverance from Egypt (Ex. 15:1–18) with the song sung by those delivered from the beast. What praise is given to God? By whom?
❑ What great and mighty deeds has God done in your life for which you will praise him today? How appropriate is the song in this passage to your experience with God? Why?
❑ What does John see next? How does the angels' attire contrast with what they are given to do?
❑ What does the temple in heaven mean: A haven of rest and a place to play harps for those who die? Or time to reckon with God's holiness and wrath unveiled in that very temple? Why?
❑ How does this passage make you feel? Why? What does it make you want to do? Why?

TO CLOSE AND PRAY / 15–30 Minutes

❑ How audible has the "praise song" in your life been this week? Like a choir of hundreds? Like a loud jazz band that has taken several breaks? Like a shy soloist?
❑ Has this study of Revelation given you a greater desire to praise God or a greater fear of the future? How do you think God wants Revelation to impact you?
❑ How can this group pray for you this week?

Notes

15:1–16:21 The seven seals have been opened (6:1–17; 8:1), the seven trumpets have been sounded (8:2–9:21; 11:14–19); now the seven bowls are about to be poured out. The bowls appear to be the content of the seventh trumpet. They may also be the third woe of 11:14.

15:1 *another great and marvelous sign.* This is the third such portent. The first was the sign of the radiant woman (12:1); the second that of the red dragon (12:3). In each case, these are events that disclose great meaning. In this case, it is the fact of divine judgment against all that is amiss in the universe. *the seven last plagues.* This is the third and final set of calamities. *with them God's wrath is completed.* This seems to mean that with the bowls, this threefold cycle of calamities has ended; God's warning to the world of the impending final judgment is complete. The concept of the wrath of God is found more often in Revelation than any other book of the Bible (e.g., 12:12; 14:10,19; 15:1,7; 16:1,19; 19:15).

15:2–4 Once more John sees an event that will, in fact, happen after the day of judgment. In this case it is a vision of the martyrs slain by the beast, standing around a heavenly sea, singing the song of the Lamb. This is a brief interlude prior to the unfolding of the events of the bowls.

15:2 *sea of glass.* That which is spread out before the throne of God (4:6). *mixed with fire.* This may refer to the fact that this is now a time of judgment; it may refer to the death of the assembled martyrs; or it may simply be a detail that has no symbolic content. *those who had been victorious.* They won over the demands of the beast (13:15–17) by refusing to disown the name of Christ; by remaining steadfast in their faith; and by refusing to worship the beast or receive his mark (14:12). They died instead and so frustrated the purposes of the beast. *harps.* Harps are instruments used in the praise of God (Ps. 81:2; Rev. 5:8; 14:2).

15:3 The first four lines of this hymn are a good example of the structural patterns of Hebrew poetry. The third line restates in different words the essence of the first line; the fourth line does the same for the second line. *the song of Moses.* There is probably only one song, not two. The song that was sung when the Israelites were delivered out of the hands of the Egyptians (Ex. 15:1–18) is of the same char-

acter (similar phrases are found in both) as the one which is sung here concerning this greater deliverance. *the song of the Lamb.* This is the song that follows. It praises God who delivered them from the beast. *Great and marvelous are your deeds.* This is a common theme in the OT (see Ps. 92:5; 111:2; 139:14). *Lord God Almighty.* God is called Almighty nine times in Revelation and only once in the rest of the NT (2 Cor. 6:18). This is appropriate, since his overwhelming power is a central feature in this book.

15:4 A rhetorical question is now raised in the first two lines of this verse. The final three lines all begin (in Greek) with "for" and cite three reasons why it is inconceivable that God is not feared and honored. *all nations will come.* The fellowship of those who belong to the Lamb includes peoples from all nations.

15:5–8 The final plagues are about to begin.

15:5 *the tabernacle of the Testimony.* This is how the heavenly temple is described. This is a reference to the tabernacle in the wilderness. It is called the "Tent of the Testimony" in Numbers 17:7 and 18:2 because this is where the two tablets were lodged that Moses brought down from Mt. Sinai (Ex. 32:15–16; Deut. 10:4–5).

15:6 Out of the temple came the seven angels with the seven plagues. The point is that the source of these impending calamities is God himself.

15:7 *bowls.* A wide, shallow drinking bowl. *who lives for ever and ever.* A reminder that although evil may seem to be overwhelming (and indeed it would be for those living under the beast), in fact, it is God alone who is eternal and who will prevail.

15:8 *filled with smoke.* When God appeared in the OT, there was often smoke (Ex. 19:18; Isa. 6:4). *from the glory of God.* At such times, no one could stand before God (Ex. 40:34–36).

UNIT 17—The Seven Bowls of God's Wrath / Rev. 16:1–21

Scripture

The Seven Bowls of God's Wrath

16 Then I heard a loud voice from the temple saying to the seven angels, "Go, pour out the seven bowls of God's wrath on the earth."

²The first angel went and poured out his bowl on the land, and ugly and painful sores broke out on the people who had the mark of the beast and worshiped his image.

³The second angel poured out his bowl on the sea, and it turned into blood like that of a dead man, and every living thing in the sea died.

⁴The third angel poured out his bowl on the rivers and springs of water, and they became blood. ⁵Then I heard the angel in charge of the waters say:

"You are just in these judgments,
    you who are and who were, the Holy
    One,
    because you have so judged;
⁶for they have shed the blood of your
    saints and prophets,
and you have given them blood to drink
    as they deserve."

⁷And I heard the altar respond:

"Yes, Lord God Almighty,
    true and just are your judgments."

⁸The fourth angel poured out his bowl on the sun, and the sun was given power to scorch people with fire. ⁹They were seared by the intense heat and they cursed the name of God, who had control over these plagues, but they refused to repent and glorify him.

¹⁰The fifth angel poured out his bowl on the throne of the beast, and his kingdom was plunged into darkness. Men gnawed their tongues in agony ¹¹and cursed the God of heaven because of their pains and their sores, but they refused to repent of what they had done.

Group Questions

TO BEGIN / 15 Minutes (Choose 1 or 2)

❏ What first-hand experience have you had with a natural disaster? What happened? What are your most vivid memories about it?

❏ What would be the worst plague for you to experience: Sores all over your body? Intense heat without air conditioning? Total darkness? Or great thirst with very little water? Why?

READ SCRIPTURE AND DISCUSS / 30 Minutes

❏ What contents are in each bowl of wrath? Why are these plagues worse than those ushered in by the trumpets (contrast, for example, 8:8 with 16:3)? What was the function of the trumpet plagues? What is the function of the plagues in this passage?

❏ Why does the angel (in charge of the waters) react to the outpouring of God's wrath, not with pain or sorrow, but with recognition of divine justice?

❏ What has God done in your life to help you repent? How receptive are you to admitting your guilt and repenting when you sin?

❏ What is described in the interlude (vv. 13–16) between the sixth and seventh bowls? What function did the frogs perform?

❏ What are the "frogs" that are battling with you? How is the battle going?

❏ How will the just purposes of God and the evil purposes of Satan finally and awfully converge at Armageddon (or "hill of Megiddo," an historic crossroads of the Middle East)? With what result (vv. 17–21)?

❏ Compare the seven seals, seven trumpets, and seven bowls to each other and to the 10 plagues of Egypt (Ex. 7–10). What examples of contrast (e.g., "not only ... but ...") can you find in each section? What is the connection between the three scenes (chronological, logical or what)? How would these scenes comfort John's original readers? How would you explain the necessity of the plagues to someone who is not a Christian?

❏ If "war is hell," could John's vision be that "hell is war"? What does this passage tell you about God's judgment?

[Scripture and Group Questions continued on page 60]

Notes

16:1–21 The whole of chapter 16 is given over to the emptying of the bowls. The parallels are clear between the plagues here and those that followed the trumpets. In each series, the first four plagues come upon earth, sea, fresh water, and heavenly bodies in that order. The fifth plagues both have to do with great pain; the sixth brought invasions from across the Euphrates. Both sets of plagues parallel the plagues in Egypt. One major difference between the trumpet plagues and the bowl plagues is their intensity. While the trumpet plagues were limited (usually they affected only a third), the bowl plagues encompass the whole. A second difference is that the first four trumpet plagues fall on the land, while the first four bowl plagues directly impact men and women.

16:1 *a loud voice from the temple.* This is most likely the voice of God, since 15:8 states that no one could enter the temple until the plagues were complete. *bowls of God's wrath.* "These plagues are not the expression of God's wrath against sin in general, nor are they punishments for individual wrongdoing. They are the outpouring of his wrath upon him who would frustrate the divine purpose in the world—the beast—and upon those who have given their loyalty to him" (Ladd).

16:2 The first plague falls upon those who bear the mark of the beast, marking them with loathsome boils. This plague parallels the sixth Egyptian plague in the OT (Ex. 9:8–11).

16:3 The second plague turns the oceans and seas into blood, killing all the sea life. This parallels the first Egyptian plague (Ex. 7:20–21) and the second trumpet plague (8:8–9). *blood like that of a dead man.* Such blood would be thick, dark, clotted and putrid.

16:4 The third plague did the same to all the fresh water. There would thus be no water to drink in the land. This parallels the third trumpet plague (8:10–11).

16:5–6 An angel breaks in on this unrelenting unfolding of tragedy in order to attest to the rightness of God in doing this.

16:5 The song in this verse closely parallels the song of the victorious martyrs in 15:3–4. It states that the judgments of God are not capricious but just. *the angel in charge of the water.* There is no other mention in the Bible of such an angel. However, in other Jewish literature, angels are in charge of natural phenomena. One such book mentions an angel who had the power to restrain the underground waters.

16:6 Yet another reason is given for the fact that God turned the waters to blood. Because they had poured out the blood of the saints, they have been given blood to drink.

16:7 Another voice affirms that the judgments of God are just. *I heard the altar respond.* This is the only time in Revelation in which the altar itself is said to speak. In 6:9 voices came from under the altar, and in 9:13 a voice came from the horns of the altar. There may be, however, some connection between these three voices. The pouring out of this wrath is, perhaps, connected to the vindication of those who have been martyred and who speak from beneath the altar (6:9–10), and to the prayers of the persecuted saints (8:3–4).

16:8–9 The fourth plague strikes the sun so that it flares up, scorching and searing people. The impact of the fourth trumpet fell on the sun, moon, and stars but it brought the opposite effect (darkness, not intense light). *they cursed the name of God.* They know full well who is behind these calamities. *they refused to repent.* Even at this point, it seems, repentance is possible. Still, they will not turn to God. Like Pharaoh, who saw the plagues and yet would not change, their hearts are hard. "They have wholly taken on the character of the false god they serve" (Caird).

16:10–11 The fifth plague directly attacks the heart of the problem. It assaults the throne of the beast and plunges his kingdom into darkness. This darkness parallels the ninth Egyptian plague (Ex. 10:21–29). *gnawed their tongues in agony.* They have no water to drink; the rivers, streams, and springs have been turned to blood. *their pain.* Probably from the scorching sun. *their sores.* The sores (which they received as a result of the first plague) continue to

[Notes continued on page 61]

Scripture (Continued)

¹²*The sixth angel poured out his bowl on the great river Euphrates, and its water was dried up to prepare the way for the kings from the East.* ¹³*Then I saw three evil^a spirits that looked like frogs; they came out of the mouth of the dragon, out of the mouth of the beast and out of the mouth of the false prophet.* ¹⁴*They are spirits of demons performing miraculous signs, and they go out to the kings of the whole world, to gather them for the battle on the great day of God Almighty.*

¹⁵*"Behold, I come like a thief! Blessed is he who stays awake and keeps his clothes with him, so that he may not go naked and be shamefully exposed."*

¹⁶*Then they gathered the kings together to the place that in Hebrew is called Armageddon.*

¹⁷*The seventh angel poured out his bowl into the air, and out of the temple came a loud voice from the throne, saying, "It is done!"* ¹⁸*Then there came flashes of lightning, rumblings, peals of thunder and a severe earthquake. No earthquake like it has ever occurred since man has been on earth, so tremendous was the quake.* ¹⁹*The great city split into three parts, and the cities of the nations collapsed. God remembered Babylon the Great and gave her the cup filled with the wine of the fury of his wrath.* ²⁰*Every island fled away and the mountains could not be found.* ²¹*From the sky huge hailstones of about a hundred pounds each fell upon men. And they cursed God on account of the plague of hail, because the plague was so terrible.*

Group Questions (Continued)

TO CLOSE AND PRAY / 15–30 Minutes

❑ How is the book of Revelation making you feel? Why? What has surprised you about God or about this book?

❑ What season are you experiencing in your spiritual life? Spring is just beginning to bud? Dead of winter? Fall is in the air?

❑ What prayer requests would you like to share with this group?

---

^a13 Greek *unclean*

Notes (Continued)

afflict them. In other words, the impact of the plagues build one upon another.

16:12–16 The sixth plague dries up the great river Euphrates. Since it is no longer a barrier, an invasion is planned (see Ex. 14:21 and Josh. 3:14–17 for other examples of God drying up water). The sixth trumpet plague was also centered on the Euphrates. This plague is different from the others in that it does not directly bring suffering to people. It does, however, pave the way for war.

16:12 *kings from the East.* The identity of these kings is unknown. One commentator noted that there have been nearly 50 different interpretations of who they are.

16:13–14 Some consider this to be a brief interlude, akin to that which was found between the sixth and seventh seals and the sixth and seventh trumpets. Others feel that it is an elaboration on the sixth plague, since the fifth and sixth events in the previous two cycles were elaborated upon. In any case, the source of miraculous power of the two beasts is explained here. It has to do with the unclean spirits that live in their mouths.

16:13 *frogs.* In the second Egyptian plague, frogs overran the land (Ex. 8:1–15). ***false prophet.*** This is the first time this name is used. It refers to the second beast in 13:11–17. Both Jesus and Paul warned about false prophets who would arise in the last days and seek to lead people astray (Matt. 24:24; 2 Thess. 2:9–10).

16:14 The frogs are identified as the "spirits of demons." In the sixth trumpet plague, demon locusts were loosed on the world. In this case, the demons cause people to follow the beast. These deceiving spirits go over to the kings of the world in anticipation of the final great battle.

16:15 A warning is interjected as the kings gather for the final, great battle. This is the voice of Jesus, repeating what he taught while he was on earth (Matt. 24:42–44; 1 Thess. 5:2; 2 Peter 3:10; Rev. 3:3), reminding the church that what is about to take place is not the final act in history. What will bring his-tory to a close and launch the new age is his personal return. They will need to remember that he is coming again for them during the difficult days ahead. ***Blessed.*** This is the third of seven beatitudes in Revelation (see 14:13).

16:16 The narrative of the sixth bowl continues. The demonic spirits gather the kings for the battle which will be described in 19:11–21. "The great conflict between God and Satan, Christ and Antichrist, good and evil, which lies behind the perplexing course of history will in the end issue in a final struggle in which God will emerge victorious ..." (Mounce). The idea of a last great battle between God's people and the forces hostile to God is mentioned throughout Scripture (Ps. 2:2–3; Isa. 5:26-30; Jer. 6:1–5; Ezek. 38; Joel 3:9–15). ***Armageddon.*** In Hebrew, this word means "the mountains of Megiddo." However, in Palestine, Megiddo is a plain that stretches from the Sea of Galilee to the Mediterranean, so it is not clear where, precisely, this is. The region of Megiddo was the site of many battles in the history of Israel (Judg. 5:19; 2 Kings 9:27; 23:29; 2 Chron. 35:22).

16:17–21 The seventh and final plague brings about the overthrow of Babylon. This was announced in 14:8 and will be described in detail in chapters 17 and 18.

16:17 *a loud voice.* Probably the voice of God (see note for 16:1). ***"It is done!"*** The calamities are over. The wrath of God has been poured out. The end is at hand.

16:19 The city of the beast is undone, as are the cities of those who aligned themselves with the beast. See 17:12–14; 18:9 for details of this event. ***God remembered Babylon.*** During the short reign of the Antichrist, it might have appeared as if God had forgotten the city and his people who lived there. But he had not. It was just a matter of time and patient endurance. Now Babylon will receive its due. ***the cup filled with the wine of the fury of his wrath.*** Babylon caused the nations to drink from the cup of her fornication and they grew rich from this adultery (18:3). Now Babylon is forced to drink from another cup—the cup of God's wrath (14:8,10).

UNIT 18—The Woman on the Beast / Revelation 17:1–18

Scripture

The Woman on the Beast

17 *One of the seven angels who had the seven bowls came and said to me, "Come, I will show you the punishment of the great prostitute, who sits on many waters. ²With her the kings of the earth committed adultery and the inhabitants of the earth were intoxicated with the wine of her adulteries."*

³Then the angel carried me away in the Spirit into a desert. There I saw a woman sitting on a scarlet beast that was covered with blasphemous names and had seven heads and ten horns. ⁴The woman was dressed in purple and scarlet, and was glittering with gold, precious stones and pearls. She held a golden cup in her hand, filled with abominable things and the filth of her adulteries. ⁵This title was written on her forehead:

MYSTERY
BABYLON THE GREAT
THE MOTHER OF PROSTITUTES
AND OF THE ABOMINATIONS OF THE EARTH.

⁶I saw that the woman was drunk with the blood of the saints, the blood of those who bore testimony to Jesus.

When I saw her, I was greatly astonished. ⁷Then the angel said to me: "Why are you astonished? I will explain to you the mystery of the woman and of the beast she rides, which has the seven heads and ten horns. ⁸The beast, which you saw, once was, now is not, and will come up out of the Abyss and go to his destruction. The inhabitants of the earth whose names have not been written in the book of life from the creation of the world will be astonished when they see the beast, because he once was, now is not, and yet will come.

⁹"This calls for a mind with wisdom. The seven heads are seven hills on which the woman sits. ¹⁰They are also seven kings. Five have fallen, one is, the other has not yet come; but when he does come, he must

[Scripture continued on page 64]

Group Questions

❏ When you were a child, what did you dream of being when you grew up? Why?
❏ If you could be famous for one hour, for what would you like to be known? Why?
❏ What bumper sticker or sign sums up your life right now? Why?

READ SCRIPTURE AND DISCUSS / 30 Minutes

❏ Who is the central figure in the next scene? Who appears to be "off stage"? In what sense is she influential? Evil? Attractive? Repulsive? Who is she (see also 14:8 and 16:19)? How are the woman and the beast like the first and second beasts of chapter 13?
❏ What here is the ultimate sin? Why?
❏ What does the angel say about the origin of the beast? Its history? Its future? What responses does the beast elicit? Why?
❏ Geographically, historically and spiritually, what do you think the beast's seven heads and 10 horns represent (see also Dan. 7:15–28)? Why do the kings and the beast join forces? With what result? How can evil turn on itself, Satan (in effect) casting out Satan? How does God's greater purpose triumph in all this?
❏ How are the readers of Revelation comforted by the various "definitions" of the symbols?
❏ In this passage, how does Babylon symbolize what is wrong in society today? For example, what institutions have been overthrown by revolution, only to be replaced by new regimes which surrender to the same godless ideology?
❏ Of society's wrongs, which ones have entrapped you from time to time? How has God enabled you to avoid the snares of "the great prostitute"?
❏ In what way do you need a "mind of wisdom" (v. 9) in your study of Revelation? In your life in the next few weeks?
❏ As you study Revelation, how frightened are you by the power of evil? How will you translate that fear into action or hope?

TO CLOSE AND PRAY / 15–30 Minutes

❏ How has your "reception" of God's voice been coming in this week? Crystal clear? Muffled but steady? Lots of static? What has he been saying?
❏ How does your participation in this group help you to hear God's voice?
❏ What can this group remember for you in prayer this week?

Notes

17–22 The end is now at hand. In the final chapters of his book, John will first describe the negative side of this event: the overthrow of the rebellious kingdom of the beast (chapters 17–18). Then he will describe the positive side: the return of the Lord and the establishment of the new heavens and the new earth (chapters 19–22).

17:1–21:8 The book of Revelation consists of four visions. The first is a vision of Christ and his letters to the seven churches (1:9–3:22). The second is a vision of seven seals, seven trumpets, and seven bowls (4:1–16:21). This is the third vision. It has three parts: the mystery of Babylon and its interpretation (17:1–18); the judgment of Babylon (18:1–19:5); and the final triumph and consummation of God's redemptive purpose (19:6–21:8) (Ladd).

17:1 For the third time, John is invited to behold a vision (1:9–11; 4:1–2, as well as 21:9–10). *sits on many waters.* The Babylon of history was built on a network of canals (Jer. 51:13). John interprets the meaning of these "many waters" in 17:15 as "people, multitudes, nations and languages." First-century Babylon is most likely Rome. "Rome could be said to be seated on many waters in the sense that she drew her strength and sovereignty from her conquest of many nations; but it will be even more true of eschatological Babylon, who will seduce all the world to worship that which is not God" (Ladd). The nature of apocalyptic writing is clearly seen here in the blending of past, present and future realities in a single symbol.

17:2 *adultery.* In this context, this term describes the corrupting influence of Babylon which enticed the nations to prostitute everything for the sake of riches and luxury (Isa. 23:16–17; Jer. 51:7; Nah. 3:4). *the inhabitants of the earth.* The people followed their rulers and joined in this orgy.

17:3 The angel then takes John into the wilderness. *in the Spirit.* John is in the midst of a vision (1:10; 4:2). *a scarlet beast.* The same beast as in 13:1, the Antichrist. His scarlet color identifies him with his master, Satan, the red dragon (12:3). It is the beast who has made the city (the harlot) great. She rides upon him. *blasphemous names.* See 13:5–6.

17:4 The woman is now described. *purple and scarlet.* The high cost of these dyes made clothing of this color expensive, so that it could only be worn by the wealthy. *gold, precious stones and pearls.* She is opulently dressed. *golden cup.* One would expect it to be filled with the finest wine. *abominable things.* Instead it contains that which is foul and detestable (Jer. 51:7).

17:5 *on her forehead.* Prostitutes in Rome wore headbands bearing the name of their owners. *The Mother of Prostitutes.* Not content simply to pursue her own adulteries, she made her daughters into harlots; i.e., she has spread her corruption throughout the world.

17:6 The beast killed the saints (13:7,15); she drank their blood. In John's day, Rome was guilty of killing Christians, but this is minor in comparison to what is seen in this vision. The true nature of the beast is revealed in this telling description.

17:7–18 The angel will now proceed to interpret the meaning of what John has seen.

17:8 *once was, now is not, and will come up out of the Abyss.* A description that mimics that of the Lamb (1:18; 2:8). "He once existed in one or more of his heads; he ceased to exist when one of the heads received a mortal wound; but he will have a future existence when the head is healed. The healing of the head will involve a satanic embodiment that will exceed anything that has yet occurred. However, this final manifestation of the beast will be short-lived; it is destined to go to perdition" (Ladd). *destruction.* Literally, perdition, the state of final doom (Matt. 7:13).

17:9 *seven hills.* Many commentators take this as proof positive that Rome (the city built on seven hills) is the identity of the beast and indeed, whatever one concludes, most likely John's readers would think of Rome. In terms of the total vision, however, "no simple identification with any single historical city is possible. The woman has formed an adulterous connection in every epoch of her history with the then existing world power" (Ladd).

[Notes continued on page 65]

remain for a little while. [11] The beast who once was, and now is not, is an eighth king. He belongs to the seven and is going to his destruction.

[12] "The ten horns you saw are ten kings who have not yet received a kingdom, but who for one hour will receive authority as kings along with the beast. [13] They have one purpose and will give their power and authority to the beast. [14] They will make war against the Lamb, but the Lamb will overcome them because he is Lord of lords and King of kings—and with him will be his called, chosen and faithful followers."

[15] Then the angel said to me, "The waters you saw, where the prostitute sits, are peoples, multitudes, nations and languages. [16] The beast and the ten horns you saw will hate the prostitute. They will bring her to ruin and leave her naked; they will eat her flesh and burn her with fire. [17] For God has put it into their hearts to accomplish his purpose by agreeing to give the beast their power to rule, until God's words are fulfilled. [18] The woman you saw is the great city that rules over the kings of the earth."

Notes (Continued)

17:10 seven kings. The identity of these kings has been hotly debated, since they cannot easily be lined up with the actual succession of Roman emperors. Some scholars take the number 7 to represent (as it often does in Revelation) the fullness of imperial power so that the seven kings stand for a succession of kingdoms. The key thing, however, is that this power is drawing to an end.

17:11 The eighth king is the Antichrist (see Dan. 7:24). This is a difficult verse with complex symbolism. A best guess is that the seventh king with the short reign will reappear a second time as the eighth king (who is therefore one of the seven) and will be a particularly virulent manifestation of the beast.

17:12 The 10 horns are identified as 10 kings (see Dan. 7:7,24). Many guesses have been made as to the identity of these 10. Most likely they "are purely eschatological figures representing the totality of the powers of all nations on the earth which are to be made subservient to Antichrist" (Beckwith). **not yet received a kingdom.** Whoever these men are, they are not Roman emperors, since they do not yet possess kingdoms. **one hour.** A short time.

17:13 They are completely devoted to the beast. They seek his ends, not their own.

17:14 They are even willing to fight against the Lamb. This final conflict at Armageddon will be discussed in 19:11–21. **because he is Lord of lords and King of kings.** Given who he is, as described in this phrase, the outcome of the battle is certain (see Deut. 10:17; Ps. 136:2–3; Dan. 2:47; Rev. 19:16).

17:15 The harlot is defined as the city which rules over many nations (see notes for 17:1). **the waters**

you saw. Babylon was located on the Euphrates River and was served by a system of canals and waterways. **are peoples, multitudes, nations and languages.** The waters are a metaphor that describes how all the nations flow into Babylon and are ruled by her.

17:16 Here John describes how Babylon is destroyed. The harlot draws her power from the beast (17:3) and, in turn, supports the beast in his plans (17:13). However, the beast—along with the 10 kings—turn on the harlot, destroying her with great viciousness (see Dan. 7:24; Ezek. 23:1–35). No reason is given for this action. **hate the prostitute.** They bear her no love for what she has done for them and to them. **leave her naked.** All her fine clothes and wonderful jewels will be taken from her (17:4). **eat her flesh.** See 2 Kings 9:30–37. **burn her with fire.** See Leviticus 21:9.

17:17 John explains this surprising turn of events. It is God who has ordered that the harlot be brought to destruction.

17:18 The harlot is the great city which dominated the world. "For John, the city is Rome. She is the wicked seducer whose pernicious influence has permeated the whole of the Mediterranean world. Yet Babylon the Great, source of universal harlotry and abomination (v. 5), is more than first-century Rome. Every great center of power which has prostituted its wealth and influence restores to life the spirit of ancient Babylon. John's words extend beyond his immediate setting in history and sketch the portrait of an eschatological Babylon; which will provide the social, religious and political base for the last attempt of Antichrist to establish his kingdom" (Mounce).

UNIT 19—The Fall of Babylon / Revelation 18:1–24

Scripture

The Fall of Babylon

18 *After this I saw another angel coming down from heaven. He had great authority, and the earth was illuminated by his splendor. ²With a mighty voice he shouted:*

"Fallen! Fallen is Babylon the Great!
She has become a home for demons
and a haunt for every evil[a] *spirit,*
a haunt for every unclean and detestable
bird.
³For all the nations have drunk
the maddening wine of her adulteries.
The kings of the earth committed adultery
with her,
and the merchants of the earth grew rich
from her excessive luxuries."

⁴Then I heard another voice from heaven say:

"Come out of her, my people,
so that you will not share in her sins,
so that you will not receive any of her
plagues;
⁵for her sins are piled up to heaven,
and God has remembered her crimes.
⁶Give back to her as she has given;
pay her back double for what she has
done.
Mix her a double portion from her own
cup.
⁷Give her as much torture and grief
as the glory and luxury she gave herself.
In her heart she boasts,
'I sit as queen; I am not a widow,
and I will never mourn.'
⁸Therefore in one day her plagues will
overtake her:
death, mourning and famine.
She will be consumed by fire,
for mighty is the Lord God who judges
her.

[Scripture continued on page 68]

---

a2 Greek *unclean*

66

Group Questions

TO BEGIN / 15 Minutes (Choose 1 or 2)

❏ When have you worked in a retail business (including selling lemonade as a child)? What did you like best about it? Least?
❏ If you were a piece of merchandise, would you be made of precious stones, fine linens, or costly woods? Why?
❏ If you could be captain of any kind of ship or boat, what kind would you want? Why?

READ SCRIPTURE AND DISCUSS / 30 Minutes

❏ As compelling as the power of evil is, a more compelling authority shouts an overriding double-edged message: one edge cutting Babylon and her followers, the other exhorting God's people. What are the two voices, the two messages, and the two responses from the two audiences? How does God's perspective on Babylon (vv. 2–6) differ from Babylon's self-understanding (v. 7)?
❏ How do the voices from the world greet the fall of Babylon (vv. 9–20)? Contemporize each of their laments—make them your own. Why do they mourn? Why would you mourn if you were in their situation?
❏ What "items of merchandise" have you bought at great price and valued highly? Which of these have been too costly because of the resulting loss in your spiritual life?
❏ Compare this passage with the following OT prophecies about the fall of the cities of Sodom and Gomorrah (Gen. 19), Babylon (Isa. 13,47), and Tyre (Ezek. 27–28). How is each an historical example of the fall of this spiritual Babylon?
❏ What conclusions do you draw concerning the destruction of Babylon from this comparison? What do you learn about God?
❏ When has an important part of your life collapsed? What did other individuals say about this demise? What perspective did God bring to your fallen situation?

TO CLOSE AND PRAY / 15–30 Minutes

❏ How heavily are sin and rebellion (either your own or the world's) weighing on you this week? Like a ton of gold and silver? Like iron weights around your ankles—constant but not paralyzing? Like just precious stones—it's a good week?
❏ How have you felt the prayers of those in this group in the past few weeks?
❏ What would you like the group to remember in prayer for you this week?

Notes

18:1–19:5 In this section the reader sees clearly John's attitude both to the eschatological Babylon and to first-century Rome. The unequivocal condemnation of Rome found here stands in contrast to the more moderate position taken toward Rome by the church earlier in the century (e.g., Rom. 13:1–7). But Rome and its attitudes to the church have changed radically in the intervening years. At first, it had afforded some protection to the fledgling church, considering it to be merely an offshoot of Judaism (which was a legal religion). All this changed under the emperor Nero, who made the Christians his scapegoats for the great fire of Rome. Succeeding emperors persecuted the church, culminating in the vicious persecution under Domitian. It needs to be pointed out, however, that "the author of Revelation is not at this point discussing how believers are to live under normal circumstances within the state. He is portraying in a prophetic manner the ultimate collapse of a monstrous antichristian world order determined to defeat the purpose of God in history" (Mounce).

18:2 The language used to describe the fall of this Babylon is similar to the language used to describe the fall of Babylon in the OT, as well as the fall of Edom and Nineveh (Isa. 13:19–22; 34:11–15; Zeph. 2:15). *"Fallen! Fallen is Babylon the Great!"* These are the very words of the second angel in 14:8 (see Isa. 21:9). *a haunt.* See Isaiah 13:21–22.

18:3 *For.* The reason for the fall of Babylon is that she has corrupted the nations of the earth. *committed adultery with her.* Adultery is a term used in the OT to describe spiritual unfaithfulness on the part of the people of Israel (Isa. 1:21; Jer. 2:20–31; 3:1; Ezek. 16:15; Hos. 2:5; 4:15). She has seduced the nations to follow the beast. What she used was the lure of riches and luxury.

18:4–5 God's people are warned against getting trapped by her seductive powers. They are urged to flee from Babylon, lest they share in her coming destruction (see Isa. 52:11; Jer. 51:45).

18:6 "A kindly spirit and love for one's enemies is one of the most significant marks of a disciple of Jesus (Matt. 5:43ff). The Christian is to bless those who persecute him and never repay evil for evil (Rom. 12:14, 17). However, this does not cancel out the final divine vindication. 'Beloved, never avenge yourselves, but leave it to the wrath of God; for it is written, "Vengeance is mine, I will repay, says the Lord" '(Rom. 12:19)" (Ladd). The theme of divine justice is found throughout the Bible (see Deut. 32:35; Jer. 50:15,29; 51:24–26; Rom. 12:19; 1 Thess. 5:15; 1 Peter 3:9).

18:7 *'I sit as queen.'* "Her fault is not mere arrogance, but an unquestioning faith in her own inexhaustible resources, unaccompanied by any sense of a deeper lack (cf. 3:17)" (Caird). *I am not a widow and I will never mourn.* Babylon is so secure in her power and invincibility that she boasts in this way. She denies that her armies will die on the battlefield. Others may experience loss, but she will not (Isa. 47:7–9). Her self-deception will end with her fall, however.

18:9–19 A great lament goes up from the kings and the merchants and the seafarers over the destruction of Babylon. These were the people who profited by their relationship with her. Their cries are not over the city herself, but over the loss of their power and profit. The cry of "Woe!" is repeated three times (18:10,16,19).

18:9 *kings of the earth.* These are not the 10 kings of 17:12–14, who are utterly loyal to the beast, and join with him in his war against the Lamb. Rather, these represent the nations of the earth who have allowed themselves to be seduced by the whore of Babylon into a life of excess. *the smoke of her burning.* Babylon has been destroyed by the beast and the 10 kings (17:16) in accord with the purposes of God (17:17).

18:12–13 The 29 items are divided into seven types of merchandise: precious minerals, fabrics used for expensive clothing, ornamental decorations, aromatic substances, food, animals, and slaves. Fifteen of the items in this catalogue of imports are mentioned in the lament over the destruction of Tyre, another great trading nation (Ezek. 27). The opulence of first-century Rome can scarcely be imagined. Suetonius, the Roman historian, writes of the emperor Caligula:

[Notes continued on page 69]

Scripture (Continued)

[9]"When the kings of the earth who committed adultery with her and shared her luxury see the smoke of her burning, they will weep and mourn over her. [10]Terrified at her torment, they will stand far off and cry:

> " 'Woe! Woe, O great city,
> O Babylon, city of power!
> In one hour your doom has come!'

[11]"The merchants of the earth will weep and mourn over her because no one buys their cargoes any more—[12]cargoes of gold, silver, precious stones and pearls; fine linen, purple, silk and scarlet cloth; every sort of citron wood, and articles of every kind made of ivory, costly wood, bronze, iron and marble; [13]cargoes of cinnamon and spice, of incense, myrrh and frankincense, of wine and olive oil, of fine flour and wheat; cattle and sheep; horses and carriages; and bodies and souls of men.

[14]"They will say, 'The fruit you longed for is gone from you. All your riches and splendor have vanished, never to be recovered.' [15]The merchants who sold these things and gained their wealth from her will stand far off, terrified at her torment. They will weep and mourn [16]and cry out:

> " 'Woe! Woe, O great city,
> dressed in fine linen, purple and
> scarlet, and glittering with gold,
> precious stones and pearls!
> [17]In one hour such great wealth has
> been brought to ruin!'

"Every sea captain, and all who travel by ship, the sailors, and all who earn their living from the sea, will stand far off. [18]When they see the smoke of her burning, they will exclaim, 'Was there ever a city like this great city?' [19]They will throw dust on their heads, and with weeping and mourning cry out:

> " 'Woe! Woe, O great city,
> where all who had ships on the sea

became rich through her wealth!
In one hour she has been brought to ruin!
[20]Rejoice over her, O heaven!
Rejoice, saints and apostles and prophets!
God has judged her for the way she treated you.' "

[21]Then a mighty angel picked up a boulder the size of a large millstone and threw it into the sea, and said:

> "With such violence
> the great city of Babylon will be
> thrown down, never to be found
> again.
> [22]The music of harpists and musicians, flute players and trumpeters, will never be heard in you again.
> No workman of any trade will ever be found in you again.
> The sound of a millstone
> will never be heard in you again.
> [23]The light of a lamp
> will never shine in you again.
> The voice of bridegroom and bride
> will never be heard in you again.
> Your merchants were the world's great men.
> By your magic spell all the nations were led astray.
> [24]In her was found the blood of
> prophets and of the saints,
> and of all who have been killed on
> the earth."

"In reckless extravagance he outdid the prodigals of all times in ingenuity, inventing new sort of baths and unnatural varieties of food and feasts; for he would bathe in hot or cold perfumed oils, drink pearls of great price dissolved in vinegar, and set before his guests loaves and meats of gold." Seutonius describes the favorite dish of emperor Vitellius (who, incidentally, spent nearly $20 million on food in one year): "In this he mingled the livers of pike, the brains of pheasants and peacocks, the tongues of flamingoes, and the milk of lampreys ..." Barclay describes the uses to which each item in this list was put. *silver.* Apparently there was a great demand for silver dishes. Some women would only bathe in silver tubs, and one general carried his silver plates into battle with him. *fine linen.* A very costly fabric, woven so fine as to be virtually transparent. It was popular in women's fashion (testifying to the immorality as well as luxury that abounded). *purple.* Purple dye was imported from Phoenicia. It was rare and expensive, since it was extracted drop by drop from a small vein in certain shellfish. *silk.* Silk came from China and was very expensive. A pound of silk was equal in value to a pound of gold. *citron wood.* A dark, luxurious wood from North Africa that was very scarce and was used to make expensive furniture. Seneca was reported to have 300 tables made from this wood, each with ivory feet. *costly wood.* This was used to make ornaments of all sorts which decorated the homes of wealthy Romans. *marble.* This was used to decorate public buildings. *cinnamon.* This spice came from South China and was used as a fragrance (Prov. 7:17). *spice.* This does not refer to spices used in cooking, but to a perfume used in the hair. *myrrh.* This was used as a medicine, as a perfume, and in embalming. *frankincense.* A gum resin from a tree used as a perfume and for flavoring wine. *wheat.* This was imported in great quantity and subsidized by the Caesars. It was distributed in Rome as a means of social control. *carriages.* These were a form of chariot used by the wealthy. *bodies and souls of men.* There was a flourishing slave trade. It was estimated that in the first century there were 60 million slaves who held jobs that ranged from the menial to the exalted. There were servants, teachers, physicians, civil servants, etc.

18:15–16a It is now the turn of the merchants to lament the loss of the great city in the same way as did the kings. This is the second dirge. *stand far off.* They lament the loss but separate themselves from city, lest they get caught in the destruction.

18:20 This song of praise from heaven stands in contrast to the lament that has just ended. The reason for such praise is that the judgment of God has come upon the city which persecuted his people. "This is not a gleeful song of personal vengeance, but an announcement of the vindication of God's justice and righteousness. It must always be kept in mind that the background for such a song of vindication is the question of whether God's rule or Satan's deceptive power is to triumph in human affairs. The time of the great tribulation (Matt. 24:21) will be a period when Satan will be allowed to do his worst ... His capital city Babylon will be drunk with the blood of martyrs (17:6). As terrible as this period is, it will be only temporary, and the destruction of Babylon will mean that God, the eternal judge, has finally given judgment for his people against Babylon." (Ladd).

18:21 It all happened so suddenly. Babylon was there in its arrogance and power and then it was gone, like a stone dropped into the sea.

18:22–23 All activity will cease in the city; neither entertainment nor work nor cooking will take place again. The houses will be darkened, festive occasions such as weddings will cease, and trading will end. *the music of harpists and musicians, flute players and trumpeters.* Babylon was known as a great patron of the arts. Flutes were used for festivals and at funerals (Isa. 30:29; Matt. 9:23). Trumpets were sounded at the games and in the theater. *millstone.* A different Greek word than that used in 17:21, this referred to the small millstone that was used in the home to grind wheat into flour for bread.

18:24 *all who have been killed on earth.* The influence of Babylon has spread throughout the land, so it can be said that in her is found the blood of all the martyrs.

UNIT 20—Hallelujah! / Revelation 19:1–10

Scripture

Hallelujah!

19 *After this I heard what sounded like the roar of a great multitude in heaven shouting:*

"Hallelujah!
Salvation and glory and power belong to
*   our God,*
²for true and just are his judgments.
He has condemned the great prostitute
*   who corrupted the earth by her adulteries.*
He has avenged on her the blood of his
*   servants."*

³And again they shouted:

"Hallelujah!
The smoke from her goes up for ever
*   and ever."*

⁴The twenty-four elders and the four living creatures fell down and worshiped God, who was seated on the throne. And they cried:

"Amen, Hallelujah!"

⁵Then a voice came from the throne, saying:

"Praise our God,
* all you his servants,*
you who fear him,
* both small and great!"*

⁶Then I heard what sounded like a great multitude, like the roar of rushing waters and like loud peals of thunder, shouting:

"Hallelujah!
* For our Lord God Almighty reigns.*
⁷Let us rejoice and be glad
* and give him glory!*
For the wedding of the Lamb has come,
* and his bride has made herself ready.*
⁸Fine linen, bright and clean,
* was given her to wear."*
(Fine linen stands for the righteous acts of the saints.)

⁹Then the angel said to me, "Write: 'Blessed are those who are invited to the wedding supper of the Lamb!' " And he added, "These are the true words of God."

¹⁰At this I fell at his feet to worship him. But he said to me, "Do not do it! I am a fellow servant with you and with your brothers who hold to the testimony of Jesus. Worship God! For the testimony of Jesus is the spirit of prophecy."

Group Questions

TO BEGIN / 15 Minutes (Choose 1 or 2)

❑ What is the greatest "win" you've seen your favorite ball team pull off? How did you celebrate?
❑ Whose wedding have you put the most time and energy into?
❑ What was the most festive wedding and reception you ever attended?

READ SCRIPTURE AND DISCUSS / 30 Minutes

❑ In contrast to the silence that comes with the fall of Babylon (18:22), what characterizes the new scene in heaven? Who participates in this praise?
❑ Compare and contrast the five songs of praise. What is the most frequent refrain? What do you learn about God's character?
❑ What are three things for which you are extremely grateful to God? Be specific. How do you usually express your gratitude to him about these things?
❑ How has your interest in worshiping God increased (or decreased) in the last year? Since beginning this study? Why?
❑ Contrast the prostitute of chapters 17 and 18 with the bride of verses 6–9 (see also Eph. 5:25–27). What do you find interesting about this contrast? Why?
❑ How is the Jewish tradition of marriage especially symbolic of the union of God's people to Christ? (See Note 19:6–10).
❑ How is John (and how might we be) tempted to worship the angel or messenger of the good news?
❑ How is the witness of Jesus related to prophecy?

TO CLOSE AND PRAY / 15–30 Minutes

❑ How does the defeat and condemnation of Babylon and the triumph and glory of the Lord God affect your overall view of your problems here and now? What is one problem you hope to manage more confidently and joyfully as a result of your study of Revelation?
❑ What actions or attitudes will you take this week in dealing with this problem?
❑ How can this group support you through prayer?

Notes

19:1 *Hallelujah!* An exclamation of praise derived from two Hebrew words meaning "Praise the Lord." It is used frequently in the Psalms (e.g., Pss. 106; 111–113), though never in the NT apart from the four occurrences in this passage (vv. 1,3–4,6). *Salvation.* Judgment alone is not the point. The fall of Babylon is a necessary part of the grand scheme of salvation.

19:2 *corrupted the earth.* The influence of Babylon had infected the whole planet. Now it is gone, and so the way has been prepared for the coming of the kingdom.

19:4 The 24 elders and the four living creatures appear for the last time in the book of Revelation. It is fitting that their last cry is "Amen, Hallelujah!"

19:6–21:8 The scene shifts again and John is witness to the final triumph of the Lamb. That which was announced in 11:15 is now enacted.

19:6–10 John announces the marriage of the Lamb, though he does not describe it. The metaphor which is used here is based on Jewish wedding customs of the first century. "First comes the betrothal. This is considered more binding than our 'engagement.' The terms of the marriage are accepted in the presence of witnesses and God's blessing is pronounced upon the union. From this day groom and bride are legally husband and wife (2 Cor. 11:2). Next comes the interval between betrothal and the wedding feast. During this interval the groom pays the dowry to the father of the bride if this has not yet been done (Gen. 34:12) ... Then comes the procession at the close of the interval. The bride prepares and adorns herself. The groom, arrayed in his best attire and accompanied by his friends, who sing and bear torches, proceeds to the home of the betrothed. He receives the bride and conveys her with a returning procession, to his own home or to the home of his parents (Matt. 9:15; cf. also Matt. 25:1 ff.) ... Finally there is the wedding feast, which includes the marriage supper. The usual festivities last seven, or even more, days ... Now the church is 'betrothed' to Christ. Christ, moreover, has paid the dowry for her [by his death on the cross] ... The 'interval' of separation has come. It is this entire dispensation between Christ's ascension to heaven and His coming again. During this period the bride must make herself ready. She arrays herself in fine linen, glistening and pure. The fine linen symbolizes her righteous acts, her sanctified character (7:13) ... At the end of this dispensation the Bridegroom, accompanied by the angels of glory (Matt. 25:31), comes to receive His bride, the Church. The wedding feast begins ... The feast lasts not one or two weeks but throughout all eternity!" (Hendriksen).

19:7 *his bride.* Israel was regularly spoken of as the wife of Yahweh (Isa. 54:5; 62:5; Jer. 31:32; Ezek. 16:8–14; Hos. 2:19–20). Jesus spoke of himself as the bridegroom (Mark 2:19–20), and John the Baptist used this same language to describe Jesus (John 3:29). Jesus also used the idea of the wedding feast in his parables (Matt. 22:1–14; 25:1–13). Paul picks up the idea of Israel as the bride of God and applies it to the church—the new Israel (Rom. 7:1–4; 1 Cor. 6:17; 2 Cor. 11:2; Eph. 5:25–27).

19:9 The focus shifts to the wedding guests. In the fluid language of metaphor, the church is both bride and guests. This same fluidity is seen elsewhere in the NT. In Mark 2:19–20, the disciples are pictured as guests at the wedding. Likewise in the parable of the wedding banquet, the bride is not mentioned. The issue there has to do with who the guests will be. However, in Ephesians 5:25–27, the church is spoken of as the bride who is made ready for her husband, Christ. *the wedding supper.* This is the great messianic banquet about which Jesus spoke (Matt. 8:11; 26:29). *Blessed.* This is the fourth of the seven beatitudes in Revelation (see 1:3; 14:13; 16:15; 20:6; 22:7,14).

19:10 *the testimony of Jesus.* This phrase is used twice. It is possible to interpret it two ways. It may refer to those who have borne witness to Jesus. The angel is in this category. If this is the correct rendering, the second time it is used it would mean that the testimony to Jesus is the substance of all prophecy. This phrase can mean, however, the testimony Jesus bore to the churches and which they held. It is used this way three times previously in Revelation (1:2,9; 12:17). If this is the case, the second use of the phrase would mean that "the message attested by Jesus is the essence of prophetic proclamation" (Mounce).

UNIT 21—The Rider on the White Horse / Rev. 19:11–21

Scripture

The Rider on the White Horse

¹¹I saw heaven standing open and there before me was a white horse, whose rider is called Faithful and True. With justice he judges and makes war. ¹²His eyes are like blazing fire, and on his head are many crowns. He has a name written on him that no one knows but he himself. ¹³He is dressed in a robe dipped in blood, and his name is the Word of God. ¹⁴The armies of heaven were following him, riding on white horses and dressed in fine linen, white and clean. ¹⁵Out of his mouth comes a sharp sword with which to strike down the nations. "He will rule them with an iron scepter."ᵃ He treads the wine-press of the fury of the wrath of God Almighty. ¹⁶On his robe and on his thigh he has this name written:

KING OF KINGS AND LORD OF LORDS.

¹⁷And I saw an angel standing in the sun, who cried in a loud voice to all the birds flying in midair, "Come, gather together for the great supper of God, ¹⁸so that you may eat the flesh of kings, generals, and mighty men, of horses and their riders, and the flesh of all people, free and slave, small and great."

¹⁹Then I saw the beast and the kings of the earth and their armies gathered together to make war against the rider on the horse and his army. ²⁰But the beast was captured, and with him the false prophet who had performed the miraculous signs on his behalf. With these signs he had deluded those who had received the mark of the beast and worshiped his image. The two of them were thrown alive into the fiery lake of burning sulfur. ²¹The rest of them were killed with the sword that came out of the mouth of the rider on the horse, and all the birds gorged themselves on their flesh.

Group Questions

TO BEGIN / 15 Minutes (Choose 1 or 2)

❏ When you were young, did you ever want a horse? Why? When can you remember first riding one?
❏ Who was your favorite fictional or real horse? Why?

READ SCRIPTURE AND DISCUSS / 30 Minutes

❏ What regarding the horse, the rider and the setting commands your attention? What description, titles and names from the rest of Revelation help you to identify the rider?
❏ Why do you think it is fitting that Christ has a name "that no one knows but he himself"? What mystery about Christ are you looking forward to understanding in heaven?
❏ Who is following Christ: The church *militant* (still on earth)? Or the church *triumphant* (now in heaven)? Why?
❏ What weapon does the rider wield?
❏ How does this supper (vv. 17–18) compare with the wedding supper (19:9)?
❏ Who are the combatants in this war (vv. 19–21)? Who wins? What happens to the enemy leaders? To the army?
❏ How does this "last battle" compare to "previous" ones (16:12–16; 17:14–16) and a "later" one (20:7–10)? What will be the final end of evil? Do you think these are different accounts of the same battle? Why?
❏ What hopes and fears does this triumphant picture bring out in you? Why? How has Jesus been your deliverer this year?

TO CLOSE AND PRAY / 15–30 Minutes

❏ If Jesus met you for supper tonight, would it be a somber or joyous time? Why? What about your life in the past week would give you sadness as you spoke with him?
❏ About what spiritual battle, or other need, can the group join with you in prayer?

ᵃ15 Psalm 2:9

Notes

19:11–21 The long-awaited event happens at last: Christ returns to deal with the powers of evil, clad as a warrior on a white horse with the army of heaven behind him. This is an event often foretold in the Bible, especially the OT (see Isa. 13:4; 31:4; 63:1–6; Ezek. 38–39; Joel 3; Zech. 14:3; Matt. 13:41–42; 2 Thess. 1:7; 2:8). The second coming of Christ is a central theme in the NT, though it is more often thought of in terms of the salvation of the saints than the destruction of evil.

19:12 *many crowns.* In contrast to the seven crowns of the dragon (12:3) and the 10 crowns of the beast (13:1), Jesus has many crowns. He is the King of kings and the Lord of lords, as the angel already revealed (17:14). The image of king is one that is strongly associated with Jesus throughout the NT (Mark 10:48; Acts 2:36; 1 Cor. 15:24–25; Phil. 2:9–11). *a name written on him.* He has already been called by the name Faithful and True (v. 11) and he will be named the Word of God in verse 13. He has a third name as well that is secret, hidden from people. In the first century, a name was considered more than merely a way of distinguishing one person from another. Names were thought to express the essence of a person. Perhaps this name expresses the essential nature of Jesus' being, which is a mystery that cannot be grasped by finite minds.

19:13 *a robe dipped in blood.* This is not his own blood. This is the blood of battle. In this passage Jesus comes not as the redeemer who dies for sins, but as the warrior who conquers evil. This parallels the image in Isaiah 63:1–6 of the figure who has the blood of his enemies on his garments. *the Word of God.* This is who John has long known Jesus to be. John begins his Gospel: "In the beginning was the Word, and the Word was with God, and the Word was God" (John 1:1). He began his first epistle in much the same way: "That which was from the beginning, which we have heard, which we have seen with our eyes, which we have touched—this we proclaim concerning the Word of life" (1 John 1:1). Jesus is the embodiment of God's ultimate word to the world.

19:14 *the armies of heaven.* This may be an army of angels or it could be an army of the redeemed as 17:14 suggests (see Zech. 14:5; Mark 8:38; Luke 9:26; 1 Thess. 3:13; 2 Thess. 1:7). In either case, the army does not engage in battle. That is left to Christ alone (v. 21). *white.* They are dressed in the garb of heaven.

19:15 Three symbols in this verse, all taken from the OT, describe the actions of the warrior. First, the weapon which he uses in this battle issues from his mouth, an image which is drawn from Isaiah 11:4 (see 1:16; 2:12,16). His sword is his word; the same word which was the source of all creation (John 1:1–3; Heb. 1:2). Second, he rules with a rod of iron, an image taken from Psalm 2:9. Such a rod speaks not of governing but of destruction. Third, he treads the winepress which is by now a familiar image in Revelation (e.g.,14:10), drawn originally from Isaiah 63:3.

19:16 *King of Kings and Lord of Lords.* This is the fourth name that is given to Christ (see Note for v. 12). This is the name by which he reveals himself to those with whom he does battle.

19:17–21 And so the battle of Armageddon begins, between Christ and the Antichrist. This is the manifestation in history of the battle fought in heaven between God and Satan (12:1–13:1). As he has done in the past (e.g., 17:6; 18:2), John does not describe the event—he simply announces that it has taken place. Following this battle, Christ will do battle with Satan (20:1–10).

19:17–18 This gruesome supper contrasts sharply with the wedding banquet of 19:6–10 (see Ezek. 39:17–20). *all people.* That is, all who bear the mark of the beast, a number which includes all kinds of people.

19:19 The enemy gathers at Armageddon. The beast is there at the head of the army, along with the kings of the earth (16:13–14,16).

19:20 The war itself is not described; only its outcome. *the fiery lake of burning sulfur.* See Note for 20:10.

19:21 The armies were slain by the sword of the rider.

UNIT 22—The Thousand Years/Satan's Doom/The Dead Are Judged / Revelation 20:1–15

Scripture

The Thousand Years

20 And I saw an angel coming down out of heaven, having the key to the Abyss and holding in his hand a great chain. *²He seized the dragon, that ancient serpent, who is the devil, or Satan, and bound him for a thousand years. ³He threw him into the Abyss, and locked and sealed it over him, to keep him from deceiving the nations anymore until the thousand years were ended. After that, he must be set free for a short time.*

⁴I saw thrones on which were seated those who had been given authority to judge. And I saw the souls of those who had been beheaded because of their testimony for Jesus and because of the word of God. They had not worshiped the beast or his image and had not received his mark on their foreheads or their hands. They came to life and reigned with Christ a thousand years. ⁵(The rest of the dead did not come to life until the thousand years were ended.) This is the first resurrection. ⁶Blessed and holy are those who have part in the first resurrection. The second death has no power over them, but they will be priests of God and of Christ and will reign with him for a thousand years.

Satan's Doom

⁷When the thousand years are over, Satan will be released from his prison ⁸and will go out to deceive the nations in the four corners of the earth—Gog and Magog—to gather them for battle. In number they are like the sand on the seashore. ⁹They marched across the breadth of the earth and surrounded the camp of God's people, the city he loves. But fire came down from heaven and devoured them. ¹⁰And the devil, who deceived them, was thrown into the lake of burning sulfur, where the beast and the false prophet had been thrown. They will be tormented day and night for ever and ever.

The Dead Are Judged

¹¹Then I saw a great white throne and him who was seated on it. Earth and sky fled from his presence, and there was no place for them. ¹²And I saw the dead, great and small, standing before the throne, and books were opened. Another book was opened, which is the book of life. The dead were judged according to what they had done as recorded in the books. ¹³The sea gave up the dead that were in it, and death and Hades gave up the dead that were in them, and each person was judged according to what he had done. ¹⁴Then death and Hades were thrown into the lake of fire. The lake of fire is the second death. ¹⁵If anyone's name was not found written in the book of life, he was thrown into the lake of fire.

Group Questions

TO BEGIN / 15 Minutes (Choose 1 or 2)

❏ What book have you most recently finished reading?
❏ If you could recommend one book, other than the Bible, as a "must read" to the nation, what would it be?

READ SCRIPTURE AND DISCUSS / 30 Minutes

❏ Why is Satan bound? By whom? How?
❏ Read Note 20:4. When and where do you think the Millennium (thousand-year reign of Christ) will begin? Why?
❏ What is the first resurrection? The second death? What do these mean to Christians? To the rest of the dead?
❏ Describe this version of the last battle, comparing it to the other versions in Revelation and to Ezekiel 38–39. What is the final fate of the beast, false prophet and Satan?
❏ Who is exempted and who is exhumed at the Great White Throne judgment? On what basis? What is the last great reality prior to the new age?
❏ What is comforting to you in this passage? Disturbing? Why?
❏ Imagine a book made of your life, with every thought and deed recorded, then read by all. How would you feel? If Christ edited that book by substituting his works for yours, how would you feel? How will you then live today?

TO CLOSE AND PRAY / 15–30 Minutes

❏ How did you do last week in dealing with the spiritual battle you shared about during prayer time?
❏ What would you like this group to pray about?

Notes

20:2 *a thousand years.* Given the symbolic use of numbers in Revelation, it is not possible to know exactly what is meant: whether a literal thousand years is intended or just "a long period of time."

20:4 This is an exceedingly difficult verse to analyze. ***thrones.*** It is impossible to know who is on these thrones beyond the fact that they will assist in the judging. Some suggest these are the apostles (Matt. 19:28), or all the saints (1 Cor. 6:2–3), or just those who overcame (3:21). ***the souls of those who had been beheaded.*** "These are the souls under the altar in 6:9 and all who are to meet a similar fate until the time of their vindication (6:11). They are called souls because at this point they are still awaiting the resurrection ... It is representative of all who gave their lives in faithfulness to their commitment to Christ" (Mounce). ***reigned with Christ a thousand years.*** The meaning of this passage has been the subject of great debate in the church. There are three main schools of thought when it comes to the Millennium (the thousand-year reign of Christ). The postmillennialists feel that the return of Christ will not occur until the kingdom of God has been established here on earth, in history as we know it. This will be the "golden age" of the church; a long reign of peace and prosperity. It will be followed by the Second Coming, the resurrection of the dead, the final judgment, and the eternal kingdom. The amillennialists do not believe there will be a literal thousand-year reign of Christ. They see it as a metaphor for the history of the church between the resurrection of Christ and his second coming, during which those believers who have died will reign with Christ in heaven. When Christ returns, there will be a general resurrection, the final judgment, and the start of Christ's reign over the new heavens and earth. They consider the binding of Satan to be what Christ did when he died on the cross (Matt. 12:29). The premillennialists believe that the events described in 20:1–6 will literally take place. Christ will return, the first resurrection will occur, and there will be a thousand years of peace in which Christ reigns here on earth. Then will come the final resurrection, the last judgment, and the new heavens and earth. The millennial reign is seen (by some) as a special reward to the martyrs of chapter 6.

20:5 *the rest of the dead.* Who these are depends on one's view of the Millennium. The premillennialist would say these are the rest of the believers (the martyrs having been raised already to reign with Christ) plus all unbelievers. Others would say that this is the resurrection of unbelievers prior to the day of judgment.

20:6 *the second death.* The first death is the death of the body; the second death involves being cast into the lake of fire (20:14; 21:8).

20:7–10 Even after a millennium of God's reign, Satan is able to gather an army of those who would oppose God and his rule. ***Gog and Magog.*** In Ezekiel 38–39, there is an extended prophecy about "Gog, of the land of Magog." As in Revelation, the final battle follows the establishment of the messianic kingdom (Ezek. 36–37).

20:9 *the city he loves.* Jerusalem. ***fire came down from heaven.*** There is no battle this time. They are destroyed by the power of God (see 2 Kings 1).

20:10 Satan joins the beast and the false prophet in the lake of fire. This is the final destination of evil in all its forms (Matt. 25:41). ***the fiery lake of burning sulfur.*** In the rest of the NT this is called Gehenna (Matt. 5:22; Mark 9:43). The Valley of Hinnom, from which this name is drawn, was a place where human sacrifice took place (2 Kings 16:3; 23:10; Jer. 7:31–32). It eventually became a kind of town dump where a fire perpetually smoldered, and thus it became a metaphor for hell.

20:12 *according to what they had done.* The idea of judgment on the basis of one's works is found in the OT and NT (Ps. 62:12; Jer. 17:10; Rom. 2:6; 1 Peter 1:17). "The issue is not salvation by works but works as the irrefutable evidence of a man's actual relationship with God" (Mounce). ***the book of life.*** Another book is opened. In it are recorded the names of those who belong to Christ (Ex. 32:32–33; Dan. 12:1; Luke 10:20; Phil. 4:3; Rev. 3:5; 13:8; 21:27).

20:13 *Hades.* This is not the same as Gehenna (see note for 20:10). It is the place where departed souls go. It was thought of as an intermediate state (Luke 16:23; Acts 2:27).

UNIT 23—The New Jerusalem Descended / Rev. 21:1-8

Scripture

The New Jerusalem

21 *Then I saw a new heaven and a new earth, for the first heaven and the first earth had passed away, and there was no longer any sea. ²I saw the Holy City, the new Jerusalem, coming down out of heaven from God, prepared as a bride beautifully dressed for her husband. ³And I heard a loud voice from the throne saying, "Now the dwelling of God is with men, and he will live with them. They will be his people, and God himself will be with them and be their God. ⁴He will wipe every tear from their eyes. There will be no more death or mourning or crying or pain, for the old order of things has passed away."*

⁵He who was seated on the throne said, "I am making everything new!" Then he said, "Write this down, for these words are trustworthy and true."

⁶He said to me: "It is done. I am the Alpha and the Omega, the Beginning and the End. To him who is thirsty I will give to drink without cost from the spring of the water of life. ⁷He who overcomes will inherit all this, and I will be his God and he will be my son. ⁸But the cowardly, the unbelieving, the vile, the murderers, the sexually immoral, those who practice magic arts, the idolaters and all liars— their place will be in the fiery lake of burning sulfur. This is the second death."

Group Questions

TO BEGIN / 15 Minutes (Choose 1 or 2)

❑ What is the best vacation you can remember taking as a child?
❑ Where is one of the most beautiful places you have ever been? What impressed you about it?
❑ What area of the world have you always wanted to visit? Why?

READ SCRIPTURE AND DISCUSS / 30 Minutes

❑ Where will the new age be lived out—on earth or in heaven? Why do you think so? How do you feel about living forever on a new earth rather than in heaven?
❑ Who will be the "residents" of the New Jerusalem? Whose presence is the vision caught up with? What, or who, is missing from this picture? Why?
❑ What is the goal of all redemption? (See Note 21:3). What do you think it will be like living without fear, pain or death and with the continual presence of God? Will this be recognizable? How so?
❑ How do you feel about seeing your body grow older in light of verse 5?
❑ What is the significance of the names ascribed to God, especially for those who "overcome" and those who do not?

TO CLOSE AND PRAY / 15–30 Minutes

❑ What has caused you mourning, sorrow or pain in the last year? In the last week? How does it help to know that this will pass away?
❑ What can you do to hold on to the perspective on suffering God gives in this passage?
❑ How can this group pray for you this week?

Notes

21:1–8 The old order is done and finished. In its place there is a new order which John announces here.

21:1 *a new heaven and a new earth.* "Throughout the entire Bible, the ultimate destiny of God's people is an earthly destiny … not in a heavenly realm removed from earthly existence" (Ladd). (See Isa. 11:6–9; 65:17; 2 Peter 3:13.) *the first earth had passed away.* This event occurred in 20:11, described by means of a few terse sentences. *there was no longer any sea.* In ancient times the sea was often pictured as dark and mysterious; it was an enemy not a friend. The lack of any seas in the new earth indicates how radically different the new will be.

21:2 *the new Jerusalem.* The new Jerusalem will be described in detail in 21:9–22:5 (see Gal. 4:26; Heb. 12:22). It was conceived of as the place where departed saints dwelt between the time of their death and the coming of the new heavens and the new earth (2 Cor. 5:8; Phil. 1:23; Rev. 6:9–11). It now descends to earth where it will finally rest. *prepared as a bride.* The church has already been pictured as the bride of Christ (see note on 19:7). John may intend the heavenly Jerusalem to be another metaphor for the church in the same way that Paul likens the church to the temple of God (1 Cor. 3:16; Eph. 2:21).

21:3 "In the Old Testament times, God's dwelling place (*skene*) first was the tabernacle in the wilderness, and later the temple; and his presence was manifested by the *shekinah* glory. In the coming of Christ, God took up his dwelling temporarily among men (John 1:14, 'the word … dwelt among us.' The same Greek root is used: *eskenosen*). During the church age, God indwells his church, which is his temple (Eph. 2:22); but this is a dwelling 'in the Spirit,' which can be apprehended only by faith, not by sight (2 Cor. 5:17). In the consummation, all this is changed; faith will be changed to sight, and 'they shall see his face' (22:4) … This is a reality which we cannot visualize; but direct, unmarred fellowship between God and his people is the goal of all redemption." (Ladd)

21:4 *He will wipe every tear from their eyes.* The suffering is over; it is finished. No longer will there need to be a call to hold on and endure. *There will be no more death or mourning or crying or pain.* All the old enemies of humanity are gone. Death itself is vanquished, so there will be no need anymore for mourning. Crying too is a thing of the past. Pain will be unknown.

21:5 *I am making everything new!* Creation, it seems, is not a static reality. Here at the end of history, God is still at work creating a new reality. That which was in principle true when an individual came to Christ, namely "If anyone is in Christ, he is a new creation" (2 Cor. 5:17), is now consummated in fact. This process also includes the physical world (Rom. 8:21). "Salvation in the biblical sense is not only the salvation of the souls of men; it includes the redemption of the body and even of their physical environment" (Ladd).

21:6 The voice from the throne (v. 3) is now identified. It is God who is speaking. This is an infrequent event in Revelation (1:8; 16:1,17). He speaks to assert that "It is done." God's plan has been realized in its fullness. *the Alpha and the Omega.* The first and last letters in the Greek alphabet. God encompasses the whole of reality—all of what can be spoken and so is. *the Beginning and the End.* He also encompasses the whole of time. *I will give to drink.* He satisfies the deepest needs—physical and spiritual—of humanity.

21:7 *he who overcomes.* This recalls the letters to the seven churches and the promises made then (2:7,11,17,26; 3:5,12,21).

21:8 The types of people who stand outside his kingdom are listed. *the cowardly.* Those who do not stand up to the beast and his demands. *the unbelieving.* "The unbelieving are not the secular pagan worlds (as in 1 Cor. 6:6; 7:12ff; 10:27; 14:22ff) but believers who have denied their faith under pressure" (Mounce). *liars.* Those people who live in falsehood.

UNIT 24—The New Jerusalem Defined / Rev. 21:9–21

Scripture

⁹One of the seven angels who had the seven bowls full of the seven last plagues came and said to me, "Come, I will show you the bride, the wife of the Lamb." ¹⁰And he carried me away in the Spirit to a mountain great and high, and showed me the Holy City, Jerusalem, coming down out of heaven from God. ¹¹It shone with the glory of God, and its brilliance was like that of a very precious jewel, like a jasper, clear as crystal. ¹²It had a great, high wall with twelve gates, and with twelve angels at the gates. On the gates were written the names of the twelve tribes of Israel. ¹³There were three gates on the east, three on the north, three on the south and three on the west. ¹⁴The wall of the city had twelve foundations, and on them were the names of the twelve apostles of the Lamb.

¹⁵The angel who talked with me had a measuring rod of gold to measure the city, its gates and its walls. ¹⁶The city was laid out like a square, as long as it was wide. He measured the city with the rod and found it to be 12,000 stadia[a] in length, and as wide and high as it is long. ¹⁷He measured its wall and it was 144 cubits[b] thick,[c] by man's measurement, which the angel was using. ¹⁸The wall was made of jasper, and the city of pure gold, as pure as glass. ¹⁹The foundations of the city walls were decorated with every kind of precious stone. The first foundation was jasper, the second sapphire, the third chalcedony, the fourth emerald, ²⁰the fifth sardonyx, the sixth carnelian, the seventh chrysolite, the eighth beryl, the ninth topaz, the tenth chrysoprase, the eleventh jacinth, and the twelfth amethyst.[d] ²¹The twelve gates were twelve pearls, each gate made of a single pearl. The great street of the city was of pure gold, like transparent glass.

Group Questions

TO BEGIN / 15 Minutes (Choose 1 or 2)

❏ What is the highest mountain you can remember being on?
❏ What is the biggest city you've been in? Would you like to live there?
❏ What is your favorite precious stone?

READ SCRIPTURE AND DISCUSS / 30 Minutes

❏ What is the first characteristic of the New Jerusalem (v. 11)? How is it constructed? What do you think is the significance of the foundations and the gates? (See Note 21:14).
❏ What is the size of the city? Of what is it constructed? Compare this vision to the related vision in Ezekiel 40:2,5; and 48:30–35.
❏ What are John and his readers meant to notice about the city in particular? Why? Considering the part of the world in which John's readers live and the conditions they were under, what would have been especially impressive about this city?
❏ What impresses you most about the city and its central figure? Why?
❏ Does the New Jerusalem fit your idea of beauty? How do you feel about the fact that the Holy City will be your hometown—that this is what Jesus has prepared for you?

TO CLOSE AND PRAY / 15–30 Minutes

❏ When in the past week have you needed a vision of the Holy City—the joyous place that awaits you?
❏ How have the people in your life, including this group, helped you to keep in mind the hope of this eternal home?
❏ How can this group pray for you this week?

---

[a]16 That is, about 1,400 miles (about 2,200 kilometers)   [b]17 That is, about 200 feet (about 65 meters)   [c]17 Or *high*   [d]20 The precise identification of some of these precious stones is uncertain.

Notes

21:9 The language used here by the angel parallels that in 17:1, where John is shown the great harlot, Babylon. The contrast between the two cities is striking.

21:10 *in the spirit.* This is the fourth vision (see 1:10; 4:1; 17:3).

21:12 *with twelve angels at the gates.* See Isaiah 62:6. *the names of the twelve tribes.* See Ezekiel 48:30–34.

21:14 *the names of the twelve apostles.* The very foundation of the city rests on the apostles of Jesus (see Eph. 2:20). The church was, of course, the result of the labors of the Twelve following the death and resurrection of Jesus. With the names of the 12 tribes at the gates and the names of the 12 apostles at the foundation, it is clear that the new Jerusalem encompasses both Israel of the Old Testament and the church of the New Testament. All of God's people have a place here.

21:16 *12,000 stadia.* It is an enormous city, beyond what any earthly city was or could be. Each of its four sides was approximately 1,500 miles long. By way of perspective, Ladd reminds us that the distance from the Dead Sea to the Sea of Galilee was only 60 miles! Of course, the numbers are symbolic. By them, John struggles to convey the vastness of the city. *high as it is long.* The new Jerusalem is a cube, as high as it is wide. The inner sanctuary of the temple was a perfect cube (1 Kings 6:20).

21:17 *144 cubits thick.* The walls were 216 feet thick. Of course, such a city would not need walls which, in ancient days, were a defense against enemies. This is God's city, and all his enemies have been destroyed. This illustrates again the fact that John is using metaphorical language. He is straining to describe that which defies description. The details of his description are not what is crucial; it is the total vision which he is seeking to express (which, in this case, is of a city so magnificent, so enormous, so secure that it can scarcely be imagined). This is the final dwelling place of God's people.

21:18 This city is built of materials unlike those used in any human city. *jasper.* This is the third time this mineral has been mentioned (4:3; 21:11; see also 21:18,19). In 21:11, such jasper was said to glow with the very radiance of God. Thus the whole city

would be aglow with God. The word jasper was used for various gem stones. The walls of the city are built of this precious stone. *pure gold as pure as glass.* Gold has long been considered very precious, and here is a city of gold! This is unlike ordinary gold, however, since it is transparent.

21:19–20 John next describes the 12 foundations of the city, each of which is decorated with a different precious mineral. These are not ordinary foundations that are hidden under the earth. These are visible for all to see. On them are written the 12 names of the apostles (v. 14). These 12 minerals are similar to eight of the 12 gems in the breastplate of the high priest (Ex. 28:17–21). The stones mentioned here are difficult to identify, because their names do not always correspond to modern gems by that name. *jasper.* A green, translucent crystal. *sapphire.* A deep blue, transparent gem. *chalcedony.* Green silicate of copper found near Chalcedon in Asia Minor. *emerald.* A green gemstone. *sardonyx.* An agate made up of layers of a red mineral by the name of sard, and white onyx. *carnelian.* Blood red. *chysolite.* Yellow topaz or golden jasper. *beryl.* A sea-green mineral. *topaz.* A greenish gold or yellow mineral. *chrysoprase.* A type of quartz which was apple-green. *jacinth.* Bluish purple. *amethyst.* Another variety of quartz; it was purple and transparent.

21:21 *twelve gates.* The gates of ancient cities were an important part of their defense. They were built into the wall, often with a tower as part of their construction. *twelve pearls.* Pearls were of great value in the ancient world (Matt. 13:45–46; 1 Tim. 2:9). The pearls from which these gates were built would had to have been enormous; again, quite beyond anything on this earth. "A rabbinic prophecy promises that God will set up in the gateways of Jerusalem gems and pearls thirty cubits by thirty in which he will hollow out openings ten cubits wide and twenty cubits high" (Mounce).

UNIT 25—The River of Life / Revelation 21:22–22:5

Scripture

²²I did not see a temple in the city, because the Lord God Almighty and the Lamb are its temple. ²³The city does not need the sun or the moon to shine on it, for the glory of God gives it light, and the Lamb is its lamp. ²⁴The nations will walk by its light, and the kings of the earth will bring their splendor into it. ²⁵On no day will its gates ever be shut, for there will be no night there. ²⁶The glory and honor of the nations will be brought into it. ²⁷Nothing impure will ever enter it, nor will anyone who does what is shameful or deceitful, but only those whose names are written in the Lamb's book of life.

The River of Life

22 Then the angel showed me the river of the water of life, as clear as crystal, flowing from the throne of God and of the Lamb ²down the middle of the great street of the city. On each side of the river stood the tree of life, bearing twelve crops of fruit, yielding its fruit every month. And the leaves of the tree are for the healing of the nations. ³No longer will there be any curse. The throne of God and of the Lamb will be in the city, and his servants will serve him. ⁴They will see his face, and his name will be on their foreheads. ⁵There will be no more night. They will not need the light of a lamp or the light of the sun, for the Lord God will give them light. And they will reign for ever and ever.

Group Questions

TO BEGIN / 15 Minutes (Choose 1 or 2)

❑ Are you a "health nut" or do you tend to eat whatever you feel like eating?
❑ What is your favorite food? Your favorite beverage?
❑ When it comes to spiritual food, what place of worship has been most satisfying in your experience?

READ SCRIPTURE AND DISCUSS / 30 Minutes

❑ Compare John's vision here with the related vision in Isaiah 60–66. What was the function of the temple in the Old Jerusalem? Why is there no need for a temple in the New Jerusalem? What speaks more clearly about God to you: The spiritual things visualized here in the New Jerusalem? Or the physical objects of the Old Jerusalem?
❑ What features will be found in the New Jerusalem (22:1–5)? Where else do we see these same features (see Gen. 1–3; Ezek. 47:1–12; Joel 3:18; Zech. 14:8)? What do you learn about God from this comparison?
❑ How easy is it for you to comprehend that this city will last forever? What does it mean to you? Does it change your lifestyle? Why or why not?
❑ How has your study of Revelation, and the many parallels to other parts of Scripture, enhanced your view of the Bible? Of the completeness of salvation? How has it affected your trust in God?

TO CLOSE AND PRAY / 15–30 Minutes

❑ Now that your study of Revelation is almost over, how do you feel about this book of the Bible? Is this different than how you felt when you began the study? How has God blessed your life through this study?
❑ What do you hope to carry with you from your time spent in the study of Revelation?
❑ You've accomplished a lot in completing the study of Revelation! What would you like to do as a group to celebrate? Plan a party? Or a dinner?
❑ What would you like this group to pray with you about in the coming week?

Notes

21:22 *temple.* The temple was the center of religious life in Israel. God was said to be present in the center of the temple, in the Holy of Holies. There is no need for a temple in the New Jerusalem because God is always present.

21:23 So radiant is the presence of God and the Lamb that the New Jerusalem has no need of artificial illumination (Isa. 60:19–20; John 1:9; 8:12). In fact, it is never night (v. 25).

21:24–26 There is a problem with the description here (see also 22:2,15). It has to do with the presence of "the nations" now that the enemies of God have been destroyed. Some speculate that this is a picture of universal salvation: "Nowhere in the New Testament do we find a more eloquent statement than this of the all-embracing scope of Christ's redemptive work" (Caird). But the problem is more apparent than real. John has simply adopted language from the prophets (as he has done throughout this section) in his attempt to convey the glory of the New Jerusalem. "The prophets were thinking mainly of a future under the historical conditions of our present life. John makes use of their sublime visions, lifting them on to the eternal plane; and at times he retains words not entirely appropriate to this new setting" (Glasson).

21:25 *on no day will its gates ever be shut.* The gates of a city were shut at night when there was the danger of a sneak attack (Isa. 60:11).

21:27 No one will have access to this utterly magnificent city unless his or her name is written in the Lamb's Book of Life.

22:1–5 The focus shifts from the city to the river of life that flows from the throne of God and of the Lamb.

22:1 The New Jerusalem is a place of eternal life. The saints will live eternally near this life-giving stream. *the river of the water of life.* The idea of such a river is a common one in the Bible (see Ps.

46:4; Ezek. 47:1–12; Zech. 14:8; John 4:10–14). *from the throne.* God is the source of life.

22:2 *middle of the great street.* The river of life is central to the New Jerusalem. *the tree of life.* The great story ends where it began, with the tree of life. In Genesis the tree of life in the Garden of Eden is lost to humanity by reason of sin (Gen. 2:9; 3:22). In Revelation it is restored. But what an awful price was paid for the sin in the intervening centuries. *twelve kinds of fruit.* See Ezekiel 47:12. *for the healing of the nations.* And indeed this is what has happened.

22:3 The curse is gone. What is left is God and the Lamb, reigning over all.

22:4 At long last too, men and women are able to behold the face of God. Gone are the intermediaries. "Throughout redemptive history, God's presence was mediated through the prophetic word, theophanies, dreams, angels and the cult. To come face to face with the living God meant death (Ex. 33:20). Jesus in his incarnation brought the presence of God to men in his own person (Matt. 1:23). ... This vision of God was still a mediated one. ... In the age to come, faith will give way to sight" (Ladd).

22:5 *And they will reign for ever and ever.* And so the story ends.

UNIT 26—Jesus Is Coming / Revelation 22:6–21

Scripture

⁶The angel said to me, "These words are trustworthy and true. The Lord, the God of the spirits of the prophets, sent his angel to show his servants the things that must soon take place."

Jesus Is Coming

⁷"Behold, I am coming soon! Blessed is he who keeps the words of the prophecy in this book."

⁸I, John, am the one who heard and saw these things. And when I had heard and seen them, I fell down to worship at the feet of the angel who had been showing them to me. ⁹But he said to me, "Do not do it! I am a fellow servant with you and with your brothers the prophets and of all who keep the words of this book. Worship God!"

¹⁰Then he told me, "Do not seal up the words of the prophecy of this book, because the time is near. ¹¹Let him who does wrong continue to do wrong; let him who is vile continue to be vile; let him who does right continue to do right; and let him who is holy continue to be holy."

¹²"Behold, I am coming soon! My reward is with me, and I will give to everyone according to what he has done. ¹³I am the Alpha and the Omega, the First and the Last, the Beginning and the End.

¹⁴"Blessed are those who wash their robes, that they may have the right to the tree of life and may go through the gates into the city. ¹⁵Outside are the dogs, those who practice magic arts, the sexually immoral, the murderers, the idolaters and everyone who loves and practices falsehood.

¹⁶"I, Jesus, have sent my angel to give you this testimony for the churches. I am the Root and the Offspring of David, and the bright Morning Star."

¹⁷The Spirit and the bride say, "Come!" And let him who hears say, "Come!" Whoever is thirsty, let him come; and whoever wishes, let him take the free gift of the water of life.

¹⁸I warn everyone who hears the words of the prophecy of this book: If anyone adds anything to them, God will add to him the plagues described in this book. ¹⁹And if anyone takes words away from this book of prophecy, God will take away from him his share in the tree of life and in the holy city, which are described in this book.

²⁰He who testifies to these things says, "Yes, I am coming soon."
  Amen. Come, Lord Jesus.
²¹The grace of the Lord Jesus be with God's people. Amen.

Group Questions

TO BEGIN / 15 Minutes (Choose 1 or 2)

❏ What breed of dog best describes your week? Why?
❏ If you could choose a few words to represent your name, what would they be?

READ SCRIPTURE AND DISCUSS / 30 Minutes

❏ What words of Christ are repeated three times in this closing (vv. 7,12,20)? How do these sum up Revelation?
❏ Regarding Jesus' claims in verses 12–17, how is the final state of humanity determined: By some arbitrary reward system, fixed from eternity? By what we have done in this present life? Or by our response to his *universal* and *undeserved* invitation to simply "come"?
❏ Is it ever too late for people to change their ways and come to Christ? Why or why not?
❏ What is the meaning of God's final curse in vv. 18–19?
❏ How have you prepared yourself for Christ's second coming? In what way has this study of Revelation helped to prepare you? How is your lifestyle in keeping with verse 7?
❏ How have your perceptions of Jesus, Satan, heaven and hell changed? Why?

TO CLOSE AND PRAY / 15–30 Minutes

❏ You've come to the close of this study. Reflecting back on the many hours spent with this group, what have you appreciated about your time together?
❏ How has each person here given something valuable to the group? Go around the group and take turns sharing about each person and their contributions.
❏ What would you like this group to remember in prayer for you in the coming weeks?

Notes

22:7–21 The final verses in the book of Revelation are in the form of an epilogue. "The epilogue consists of a group of exhortations and affirmations loosely strung together which authenticate the prophecy, assert the certainty of the Lord's coming, and bid his readers to heed the words of his prophecy" (Ladd). It is mostly a reiteration of what has already been said.

22:7 Jesus affirms what he said at the beginning of the book (2:16; 3:11). In light of this fact, his people must always be alert, always prepared for his return. *coming soon.* See 1 Corinthians 7:29–31; 1 Thessalonians 4:15. *Blessed.* This is the sixth beatitude. *keeps the words of prophecy.* The aim of the book is not so much to inform the church about the details of the last days as it is to call the church to faithful living in the midst of the struggle it faces with evil.

22:8 As he did at the beginning of the book (1:1,4), here at the end John identifies himself. All that is necessary is a single name, John. The church knows who he is. *saw and heard these things.* This book is the record of visions John had. He did not create this out of his imagination; nor is it a literary creation derived from the OT. He put down in words what was revealed to him.

22:10 *the time is near.* Once again, he reiterates that the Second Coming is drawing near. Jesus did not, of course, return in the first century. The question is, therefore, what this phrase means. F.F. Bruce feels that "the end is always near in the sense that each successive Christian generation may be the last. ... One of the more helpful suggestions is made by Ladd who holds that the Apocalypse has a twofold perspective: it is primarily concerned with the struggle between Christ and Antichrist which comes to a climax at the end of the age, but this struggle also existed between church and state in the first century and has surfaced in history whenever the state has made totalitarian demands. Thus the time has always been at hand." (Mounce).

22:14 *Blessed.* The final beatitude in the book of Revelation. *wash their robes.* An allusion to 3:4 and 7:14. Those who are blessed are those who, by faith, have participated in the redeeming death of Jesus.

22:16 Jesus speaks again, attesting to the authenticity of this book. He reiterates what was said in 1:1—that this vision has come from Jesus to the angel to John to the churches. *the Root and Offspring of David.* He is the messianic King from the line of David (Matt. 1:1; 9:27; 15:22; 21:9; Rom. 1:3; Rev. 5:5). The image of a shoot that grows out of the stump of David is taken from Isaiah 11:1. *the bright Morning Star.* See Numbers 24:17.

22:17 There are two ways to read this verse. It can be understood to contain two invitations. In the first invitation, the Spirit, the Bride, and the hearers of this book beckon Jesus to return. In the second invitation, all who wish are invited to partake of the tree of life (22:12,20). But reading it this way makes the transition very abrupt from one invitation to the other. It is probably better to read the whole verse as an invitation to the world. What an amazing picture this is: the Holy Spirit, the church, and all who read this book beckoning the world to come to that which will give them true life.

22:18–19 A warning is affixed to the book. No one is to tamper with its contents, either to add to it or take away from it (Deut. 4:2). This would be a real temptation with a book like this, whose message is mysterious, harsh at times, and often hard to understand. The temptation would be to leave out or explain away the parts that do not conform to one's views. Or one might be tempted to add other prophecies and give them the same status as these. *his share in the tree of life.* The second part of the warning (about taking away) is addressed specifically to those who are believers.

22:21 For the third time in this epilogue, the reader is reminded that Jesus is coming soon. *Amen. Come, Lord Jesus.* John's response to this declaration is: "So be it; let it happen; Come Lord Jesus." "The longing for the Lord's coming stands at the heart of the Christian faith; apart from Christ's return, his redemptive work remains forever incomplete. His return is the only sure hope for the future of the world" (Ladd).

AUTHOR'S NOTES

To write notes for the book of Revelation is a formidable task; it is, in fact, an impossible task. For one thing, there is no consensus as to how this piece of writing ought to be interpreted. Furthermore, "Apocalyptic" as a literary genre is an unfamiliar form for us in the twentieth century. We simply do not know how to handle it properly. This is further complicated by the fact that the symbol system used in Revelation is too remote from us to analyze easily. Then there is the fact that there are strong exegetical schools that insist upon a particular line of interpretation. However, to follow one tradition is automatically to violate another tradition. It is just not possible to write notes for Revelation that will satisfy everyone. Nor is it possible to write notes that capture accurately the full sweep and grandeur of the vision presented in this book. Thus these notes are offered with a profound sense of tentativeness. They are akin to a "best guess."

Yet, having said this, it must also be stated that this is the nature of vision and symbol. It cannot be captured cognitively. By its very nature, it has the power to suggest multiple meanings. The notes seek to define the general boundaries of the symbols; the readers, however, must open themselves to the material on their own and let it work its wonder on them. The book of Revelation is as much God's word as the Gospel of Mark or the epistle to the Ephesians and will, with patience, open up to us the ways of God, despite the difficulties of interpretation or the strangeness of the landscape.

This is not to say that all is murky in this last book of the Bible. The grand themes are abundantly clear: God is in control; history is going someplace; evil will be dealt with; there is a glorious future for God's people. Trying to read this through the experience of those suffering, first-century Christians to which it was written, one can almost taste the strong flavor of hope that it gave them. Life around them is not out of control.

God is mighty and powerful—in the end he will prevail. Evil may appear to have a way over them, but its power is finite and will come to an end. Evil is to be resisted, even to the point of death. God's people will have to suffer and die, but this is not the last word; they will reign in heaven where they will experience a blessed rest. History is not out of control—there is corruption and seduction to be sure, but God is the master of time and eternity. History will one day draw to a close. A new heaven and a new earth

are coming. It is the Lamb of God who will bring all this to pass.

These themes are large, so large in fact that their very boldness may cause us to miss them. This is a book of symbols. We dare not get bogged down in the futile struggle to match historical events to specific symbols, and in the minutia and hopelessness of the task miss the profound meaning of the book.

And it is also true that although it is not possible to pin down in strict chronology the events at the end of history (Revelation gives a set of snapshots of the various events, not a consecutive history of them), the key incidents and their order are clear. It all begins with the murmuring that the end is coming—strange and troubling events take place. These "troubles" grow in intensity until the Great Tribulation is upon the world. Evil reigns in a virulent way for a short time. The church is assailed, suffering is great, martyrdom frequent. But then Babylon is cast down and the day of salvation draws near. Jesus returns and does battle with the Antichrist; the Day of Judgment takes place; and the New Jerusalem descends. Thus a whole new age begins—one which spans eternity and in which the people of God live in his presence while the water of life flows through the center of the city.

The analytic approach that has been followed combines what have been called a preterist and a (moderate) futurist method of interpretation. Revelation is understood to speak both to the immediate first-century situation as well as to the great eschatological events in the future. And like OT prophecy which preceded it, it blends together, both the immediate and the future, without concern for chronology. The beast in chapter 13 is both Rome (the oppressing Imperial power in the first century) and the Antichrist who will function at the end of time.

I made an interesting discovery while working on these notes. Most of the material written about Revelation has been done by left-brain, cognitive-oriented scholars, whereas Revelation is basically a right-brain, affect/image-oriented book. You will find the same problem with these notes. The format for this series is definitely left-brain.

Special thanks to my assistant, Christopher Smith, who read over these notes and offered many helpful comments (most of which have been incorporated into the final draft), drawn from his own extensive study of this book.

ACKNOWLEDGEMENTS

The following materials have been used in writing these notes. Of special importance are two books: *A Commentary on the Revelation of John,* George Eldon Ladd, Grand Rapids, MI: Wm. B. Eerdmans Publishing Co., 1972; and *The Book of Revelation* (The New International Commentary on the New Testament), Robert H. Mounce, Grand Rapids, MI: Wm. B. Eerdmans Publishing Co., 1977. I have relied heavily on these two sources, as the quotations in the notes indicate. I was most comfortable with their approach to the analysis of the text; not surprisingly, since Dr. Ladd was a professor of mine when I was in seminary and Dr. Mounce acknowledges his debt to Ladd (and two others) for his own interpretive approach. The reader is encouraged to consult these commentaries and make use of their thorough analysis of the book of Revelation.

Reference was also made to: *The Revelation of John,* 2 vol., William Barclay, Philadelphia: Westminster Press, 1960; *The Book of Revelation* (The New Century Bible Commentary), G. R. Beasley-Murray, Grand Rapids, MI: Wm. B. Eerdmans Publishing Co., 1974; *The Apocalypse of John,* Isbon T. Beckwith, Grand Rapids, MI: Baker Book House, reprint 1967; *The Revelation of St. John the Divine* (Harper's New Testament Commentaries), G. B. Caird, San Francisco: Harper & Row, 1966; *A Critical and Exegetical Commentary on the Revelation of St. John* (The International Critical Commentary), R. H. Charles, Edinburgh: T & T Clark, 1920 (2 vols.); *The Revelation of John* (The Cambridge Commentary), Thomas F. Glasson, Cambridge: University Press, 1965; *More Than Conquerors: An Interpretation of the Book of Revelation,* William Hendriksen, Grand Rapids, MI: Baker Book House, 1940, 1967; *The Revelation of St. John* (Tyndale New Testament Commentaries), Leon Morris, Grand Rapids, MI: Wm. B. Eerdmans Publishing Co., 1981; *I Saw Heaven Opened: The Message of Revelation* (The Bible Speaks Today), Michael Wilcock, Downers Grove, IL: InterVarsity Press, 1975.

PERSONAL NOTES

PERSONAL NOTES